## YES!

It is possible to be dirty (sort of) and funny (hilarious, yet) at the same time. Of course, what's mildly risqué to one person may be bawdily offensive to another individual. That's the funny thing about humor. And Larry Wilde is that rare genius of a comedian who can hit you with an ethnic, political, religious, or sexy punch line . . . and make it a funny experience.

This collection of naughty humor ranges from the gentle rib-tickler to what we feel is wildly hysterical. The theme is, of course, off-color . . . jokes your maiden aunt would swoon from . . . stories they crack up with in the locker room. But all guaranteed to prompt a laugh. Just open this book to any page and see if *you* can resist!

**Books by Larry Wilde**

*The Official Polish/Italian Joke Book*
*The Official Jewish/Irish Joke Book*
*The Official Virgins/Sex Maniacs Joke Book*
*The Official Black Folks/White Folks Joke Book*
*MORE The Official Polish/Italian Joke Book*
*MORE The Official Jewish/Irish Joke Book*
*The Official Democrat/Republican Joke Book*
*The Official Religious/NOT SO Religious Joke Book*
*The Official Smart Kids/Dumb Parents Joke Book*
*The Official Golfers Joke Book*
*The LAST Official Polish Joke Book*
*The Official Dirty Joke Book*
*The Official Cat Lovers/Dog Lovers Joke Book*
*The LAST Official Italian Joke Book*
*The Official Book of Sick Jokes*
        and
*The Complete Book of Ethnic Humor* (Corwin Books)
*How The Great Comedy Writers Create Laughter*
    (Nelson-Hall)
*The Great Comedians* (Citadel Press)

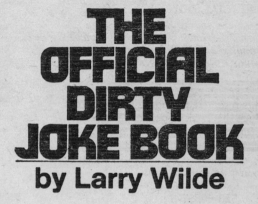

# THE OFFICIAL DIRTY JOKE BOOK

## by Larry Wilde

PINNACLE BOOKS    LOS ANGELES

# THE OFFICIAL DIRTY JOKE BOOK

An original Pinnacle Books edition, published
for the first time anywhere.

ISBN: 0-523-40687-8

First printing, January 1978
Second printing, May 1978
Third printing, September 1978
Fourth printing, December 1978
Fifth printing, November 1979
Sixth printing, August 1980

Cover illustration by Ron Wing

*Printed in the United States of America*

PINNACLE BOOKS, INC.
2029 Century Park East
Los Angeles, California 90067

To my literary agent, Jane Jordan Browne —who has such a clean mind she had to invite the neighborhood Peeping Tom in to explain these jokes.

## ABOUT THE AUTHOR

| | |
|---|---|
| Hair: | Black |
| Eyes: | Brown |
| Nose: | Bobbed |
| Weight: | Too much |
| Height: | 1.83 meters |
| Age: | Aquarius |
| Home town: | Jersey City, New Jersey |
| Alma Mater: | University of Miami, Florida |

| | |
|---|---|
| Residence: | Los Angeles |
| Married: | Definitely |
| Children: | None to speak of |
| Occupation: | Comedian |
| Habitat: | Television, nightclubs, hotels, weddings, bar mitzvahs, meat market openings |
| Hobbies: | Sex/golf |
| Avocation: | Author |
| Books in print: | Thirteen |
| Ambition: | Hold National Joke-Off Contest to choose the best amateur storyteller |

# CONTENTS

# SUPER STUDS

*Sex symbols * Sassy singles * Skirt Chasers * Sack Scorers * Snow-Job Sharpies * Snatch Scroungers*

\*    \*    \*

"How would you like to wind up the evening at my apartment listening to some records?" asked Arthur.

"Do you promise that we'll just listen to records?" countered Cora.

"I promise."

"And if I don't like the records?"

"Then you can get dressed and go home."

\* \* \*

# STUD

*A man who can get his hands on women without having them on his hands*

*Foxy Chick:* Would you help a young girl in trouble?

*Smooth Stud:* Sure. What kind of trouble would you like to get into?

\* \* \*

Loretta lowered her lashes and whispered, "Kiss me goodnight."

So Bob kissed her on the navel.

"Why did you do it there?" she asked with surprise.

"Oh," he answered, "I wanted to see what you'd open first—your eyes or your legs."

\* \* \*

Walt was being interviewed for a job and the man who was probing his psycho-stability said to him, "Do you think sex is dirty?"

"Yes, I do," answered Walt, "*if* you do it right!"

\* \* \*

Charlie was chatting with his socialite girlfriend's flirtatious mother. "If my daughter and I were both drowning and you came along," teased the woman, "which one of us would you rescue first?"

4

"You, of course," answered Charlie. "I've already *had* your daughter!"

\* \* \*

## OPTIMISTIC STUD

*A guy who makes a motel reservation before he sees his blind date*

\* \* \*

"I don't think you enjoyed me," she pouted.

"Of course I enjoyed you," he grinned. "Didn't you hear me laughing?"

\* \* \*

One Hell's Angel remarked to another, "I don't see you at the Gang Bangs anymore. What happened?"

"I got married," said his buddy.

"No shit, man!" said the first cycler, "is legal tail any better than the normal kind?"

"It ain't even as good," said the new groom. "But you don't have to stand in line for it."

5

*She:* Kiss me!

*He:* At a time like this, you're asking me to change positions?

\* \* \*

"Hey, wise guy," complained the delightful dish. "What's the big idea? You promised you'd take me to Florida!"

"I said nothing of the sort," insisted her gentleman friend. "I merely commented that I was going to Tampa with you."

\* \* \*

## MACHO MAXIM

*Next to a beautiful girl, sleep is the most wonderful thing in the world.*

\* \* \*

"You're gorgeous," breathed Ray to the well-built blonde in his arms. "Your skin is so soft, your lips so smooth, your . . ."

"Flatterer," she gasped, "where did you learn to talk to a woman that way?"

"At the factory where I'm foreman," said Ray. "It helps to increase production."

6

# OVERHEARD AT AN X-RATED MOTEL

"What do you mean I talked you into it? All I did was clear my throat."

* * *

Andy was approached by the artificial-insemination division of a family-planning group to contribute to a public sperm bank.

"No, I'm sorry," he said, "but I give the United way."

* * *

Then there was the unreconstructed male supremacist who said that if all the women's lib activists were laid end to end, that would be the best thing that could happen to them.

* * *

Allen faced his fiancée. "Before we get married, I want to confess about some affairs I've had in the past."

"But you told me about those a couple of weeks ago," answered his girl.

"Yes, darling," he explained, "but it's the past two weeks I'm talking about."

*A sneaky young bachelor named Lodge*
*Had seat belts installed in his Dodge.*
*Once a broad was strapped in*
*They could commit sin*
*Without even leaving the g'rage.*

\*    \*    \*

## STUD BOOK

*A male order catalog*

\*    \*    \*

A recent survey of male sexual practices revealed that after intercourse:

Twenty percent rolled over and had a cigarette.

Two percent washed.

Three percent went to the refrigerator for a snack.

Seventy-five percent got up, dressed, and went home.

\*    \*    \*

Mickey and Spike, two bus drivers, were in the locker room getting dressed after finishing their daily route. "What time did you pull out this morning?" asked Mickey.

"I didn't," answered Spike, "and I'm worried about it."

Did you hear about the stud who has labeled his little black book *Future Shack?*

*    *    *

Carl came over and asked his buddy Fred to return the girl he had borrowed a week ago. Fred said, "Do you need her badly?"

Carl replied, "It's not for me, it's for the guy I borrowed her from. He says the fella who's married to her wants her back."

*    *    *

*Paul:* What do you give a girl who has everything?

*Saul:* A trip to the gynecologist so she can keep it in good condition.

*    *    *

Two beauty pageant judges were watching the girls parade by.

"Did I understand you to say," inquired the elderly judge, "that you'll automatically vote for the girl who doesn't appear to have a chance?"

"That's not quite it," explained the younger man. "What I said was that I invariably vote for the sleeper."

9

# STUD'S STANDARD

*Never put off until tomorrow*
*what you can put in tonight.*

\*    \*    \*

"Did you hear about Harry?"
"No."
"He's decided to devote his life to help-
ing morally handicapped girls."

\*    \*    \*

A swimming race was held in New
York's East River. Barrows, a powerfully
built truck driver, favored to win, never
even finished.
"What happened?" asked his buddy.
"I saw this great lookin' chick dangling
her legs from the dock, I got an erection,
and it anchored me to the riverbed."
"Why didn't you turn over and float?"
"What would I have done when I came
to the Brooklyn Bridge?"

\*    \*    \*

Did you hear about the guy who was an
incurable romantic until penicillin came
along?

Some California beach boys have formed a Super Stud Club. These are the entrance requirements: "All applicants must strip and crawl on the beach on their hands and knees. Those who do not leave five trails are rejected."

*　*　*

Gunther stopped his buddy, Bryan. "Hey, you got a match?"

Bryan turned out all his pockets. He produced half a dozen tins of aspirin but no matches.

"Whatsa matter, headache?"

"No," said Bryan, "every drugstore I went to—women attendants."

*　*　*

## SCORE PAD

*A bachelor's apartment*

*　*　*

Stan spied her over in the corner. After chatting for a few moments, he said, "Let's go for a walk in the garden."

"I can only spare a minute," she said.

"That's all right," said Stan," I'm an efficiency expert."

A fire broke out in a suburban hotel, and the frightened guests scrambled out, covering themselves with whatever they could grab as they fled their rooms. Deliciously built Dorothy dashed out in the nude, and in her excitement, continued to run until exhausted. Too tired even to walk, she stood by the road hoping for a ride.

A man on a bicycle came along and offered her a lift, which she gladly accepted. They rode for some distance without conversation, when she finally said, "You're not very observant. Didn't you notice that I'm not wearing anything?"

"Ah," he replied, "you're not very observant yourself. Didn't you notice that this is a girl's bicycle?"

*"This is a girl's bicycle!"*

In Manhattan Rob, a seventeen-year-old youth, was hauled into court for brawling.

"State your case!" the judge ordered the youth.

"It happened this way," explained the boy. "I was in the phone booth peacefully talking to my girl, Dotty, when along comes this guy who decided he wants to make a phone call. So he grabbed hold of me and tossed me out on my ear."

"Can't blame you for losing your temper," mused the judge.

"As if *that* wasn't bad enough," Rob continued, "he had the nerve to grab hold of Dotty and throw her out, too!"

\* \* \*

*Clark:* I went fishing with my new girl.
*David:* Catch anything?
*Clark:* I'll know in a few days.

\* \* \*

Fifteen-year-old Bobby was running out of a theater where he had just seen a porno movie.

The manager stopped him. "Why are you in such a hurry?" he asked.

"My mother told me," said Bobby, "that if I ever looked at anything bad I would turn to stone—and I've started!"

14

# STUD'S SONNET

*A real bosom pal*
*Is a pretty gal*
*With mammary glands*
*That will fill both hands.*

\*　　\*　　\*

Hazel and Betty were in the back row of a theater watching *Deep Throat*. Suddenly, Hazel leaned over and whispered to her friend, "The guy sitting next to me is masturbating!"

"Well," said Betty, "tell him to stop!"

"I can't," said Hazel. "He's using my hand!"

\*　　\*　　\*

*Sure, candy is dandy, but sex won't rot*
*your teeth.*

\*　　\*　　\*

"Hey, turn about is fair play!" grinned the handsome lab technician when he visited the perky massage-parlor girl. "Remember me from the clinic last week? I'm the guy who pricked your finger!"

15

In a Chicago hotel where the lingerie manufacturers were holding their annual convention, George talked Roberta, one of the models, into coming to his room.

"How about a little something?" he asked.

"Wait a minute," said the girl. "I'm just a poor working stiff. Give me fifty bucks and I'll take real good care of you."

"All right," said George. "But on one condition."

"What's that?"

"Let me turn out the lights and do it to you as many times as I want and take all the time I want."

Roberta agreed. Two hours later she whispered in his ear, "Gee, you're screwing better than ever, George."

"George, hell!" cried the guy who was on top of her. "I'm just one of his friends. George is out in the corridor selling tickets!"

\* \* \*

The aging hardcore skin-flick actor arrived home dog-tired. "Did you have a hard day at the studio, baby?" asked his girlfriend as she handed him a drink.

"Yes, thank God!" he replied.

Chuck and his girl spent a fun evening in the park just petting. Now they were running to catch the last bus. "Put your fingers in your mouth and whistle to the driver!" suggested the girl.

"Not on your life!" replied Chuck. "I'd rather walk!"

*     *     *

## PROFESSIONAL STUD

*A working stiff*

*     *     *

A well-dressed man of about forty, carrying a briefcase, boarded an airplane and selected a seat next to a little old lady.

He placed the briefcase at his feet, opened it, took out a picture of a nude girl and pinned it on the back of the seat in front of him. He then reached into his pocket and took out a handkerchief, zipped down his fly, and took out his pecker. After playing with himself until orgasm, he wiped it off, zipped himself up, put the handkerchief back in his pocket, and put the picture back in his briefcase.

He then looked at the old lady and asked, "Do you mind if I smoke?"

Pretty Peggy approached the secluded lake after looking about carefully, slipped out of her clothes, and was about to plunge into the water when the sheriff appeared.

"Pardon me, miss," he said, "but swimmin' ain't allowed in this lake."

"Why didn't you tell me before I got undressed?" she exclaimed, blushing furiously.

"Well," said the sheriff, "there ain't any law against undressing."

*"Ain't no law against undressing!"*

# STUD'S SOPHISTRY

*Girls on the pill*
*Most frequently will*

\* \* \*

Big Bart ran into a buxom blonde he had met casually at a bar a few night before.

"Great seeing you again," he said. "It just happens there's a groovy party happening tonight and I'd like you to come. I won't take no for an answer."

"Where's it at?" asked the pretty doll.

"At my house, baby, and it's gonna be a gas. Lots of liquor, music, and sex. And it could last all weekend."

"Sounds good," said the girl eagerly. "Who's all going to be there?"

"Oh," said Big Bart, "just you and me."

\* \* \*

A young athlete went back to a drugstore three times in the same evening and bought a dozen rubbers each time. "What's the matter?" asked the druggist, "are you ripping them?"

"No," said the youth. "I decided to stay all night!"

"Freddie is a self-made expert in lady's fashions."

"How's that?"

"Every time his girl buys a new bra he insists on having a hand in it."

\* \* \*

Nancy the nympho was getting all the particulars from a potential new boy-friend. In between kisses she asked about his dimensions.

"I'm six feet seven, I weigh two hundred forty pounds, and I have a fifty-nine-inch chest and a twenty-eight-inch waist."

"Wow! You pass!" whispered Nancy. "Now tell me how long the instrument of delight is."

"Four inches!"

"Oh," sighed Nancy, disappointedly. "Four inches."

"Yeah," he said, "when it's relaxed, it's four inches—from the floor!"

\* \* \*

## STUD

*A man who sells retirement plans for girls*

"My beautiful foxy lady," whispered the suave dude, "you're the only chick for me. I dig you, I'm crazy 'bout you, I'm nuts 'bout you. I can't make it through the night without your love."

"Hey, wait a minute," protested the bashful girl. "I don't want to get serious."

"Hell, baby," he queried, "who's serious?"

\* \* \*

*A stud feels perked*
*And truly chipper*
*When he meets up with*
*A cooperative zipper.*

\* \* \*

*Bill:* I think I'm starting to walk in my sleep.
*Will:* What makes you think that?
*Bill:* I woke up in my own bed this morning.

\* \* \*

"My mother," cooed the cute young new receptionist, "says there are some things a girl should not do before twenty."

"Your mother is right," said the office manager. "I don't like a large audience either."

"I'd like to buy some body make-up for my girlfriend," the young musician told the clerk at the cosmetics counter.

"Certainly, sir," said the clerk. "What color would you like?"

"Never mind the color," said the musician. "What flavors do you have?"

\* \* \*

Keith and Roy, clothes connoisseurs, were discussing men's fashions. "I trust my tailor implicitly," remarked Keith. "He's great!"

"I bow to my tailor's daughter," replied Roy. "She's the only thing he ever made that fits me."

\* \* \*

There was a young fellow named
    Lancelot
Whom the neighbors all looked on
    askance a lot.
  For whenever he'd pass
  A presentable lass,
The front of his pants would advance
    a lot.

# TODAY'S ALL-AMERICAN BOY

*A young fellow who eats both Mom's
apple pie and the girl next door.*

\* \* \*

"How did this accident occur?" asked the
doctor.

"Well," explained the patient, "I was
making love to my girl on the living-room
rug when, all of a sudden, the chandelier
came crashing down on us."

"Fortunately, you've only sustained
some minor lacerations on your buttocks,"
the doctor said. "I think you're a very
lucky man."

"You said it, doc," explained the man.
"A minute sooner and it could have frac-
tured my skull."

\* \* \*

Did you hear about the super stud who
recruited girls for the sexual revolution
and then spent the first three weeks drill-
ing the platoon?

\* \* \*

"I saw that X-rated movie mystery."
"Who did it?"
"Everyone!"

Walking up to the hardware store clerk, the attractive female asked, "Can you give me a screw for a doorknob?"

"Sure," replied the clerk, "and if you're good, I'll buy you dinner besides."

* * *

Fran's fine figure had been poured into a beautiful form-fitting gown, and she made a point of calling her date's attention to it over and over again throughout the evening.

Finally, over a nightcap in his apartment he said, "You've been talking about the dress all evening long. You called my attention to it first when we met for cocktails, mentioned it again at dinner, and still again at the theater. Now that we're here alone in my pad, what do you say we drop it?"

* * *

## STUD

*A man with a little black book of cancelled chicks*

* * *

"Hey, is all this kissing healthy?"

"Honey, there may not be many vitamins in a kiss but it's a great bone builder."

On a balmy spring evening Austin took his girl Rita out for a ride in the country in his new Volkswagen. While they drove, she cuddled and fondled him and kissed his neck and blew in his ear.

Soon they reached a secluded spot. Rita got out, walked over to a tree and awaited Austin. But he didn't follow her. Finally, she called out: "Honey, if you don't hurry up, I'll be out of the mood!"

"Hell," he answered, "if I don't get out of the mood, I won't get out of this Volkswagen!"

"*I can't get out of the car!*"

Mike had just moved into his apartment and decided he should get acquainted with his across-the-hall neighbor. When the door was opened he was delightfully surprised to see a beautiful young blonde bulging out of a skimpy see-through negligee. Mike looked her squarely in the eye and ad-libbed:

"Hi, I'm your new sugar across the hall—can I borrow a cup of neighbor?"

\* \* \*

## A QUICKIE

*No sooner spread than done*

\* \* \*

While questioning a suspect, the police detective leafed through the man's folder. "I see here," he said, "that you have a string of previous arrests. Here's one for Armed Robbery, Breaking and Entering, Sexual Assault, Sexual Assualt, Sexual Assault . . ."

"Yes, sir," replied the felon modestly, "it took me a little while to find out what I do best!"

A couple of drunks in a bar started talking about sex. "Say," said the first one, "have you ever gotten so drunk you kissed a broad's navel?"

"Drunker!" answered his pal.

\* \* \*

## COCKTAIL CONVERSATION

"I'm a man of few words. Will you or won't you?"

"Your apartment or mine?" said the chick.

"Look," he said, "if there's going to be such a lot of discussion about it, let's forget the whole damn thing."

\* \* \*

Unable to manage his rebellious girlfriend Walter asked his dad how he had dealt with similar problems. "Well, son," replied the father, "every time your mother began to act up, I'd take down her pants and spank her."

"I tried that," said Walter, "but by the time I get my girl's pants down, I'm not mad at her anymore."

A group of guys were exchanging their opinions about the opposite sex. They agreed there were "chest-men," "leg-men," etc. "What is the first thing you notice about a girl?" one of them asked.

Said the other, "It depends on which way she's going."

\* \* \*

## STUD'S APARTMENT

*Wildlife sanctuary*

\* \* \*

When the subject of reincarnation came up at a bar, the boys took turns telling how they would like to come back.

"I'd like to be reincarnated as a whale," announced Tony.

"Whale?" someone asked. "Why in heaven's name a whale?"

"Just think how much I'd be in demand," he replied, "if I were able to breathe through the top of my head."

\* \* \*

# GAY DECEIVERS

*Guys * Goys * Greeks * Gobblers *
Gangs * Gooses*

*       *       *

"Gosh, you have beautiful bosoms."
"You just say that 'cause you're an over-sexed deviate."
"No, I really mean it, Chester!"

* * *

# WANTON WANT AD

*Mature, respectable businessman seeks equally responsible man to share home and living expenses. Send character recommendations, credit references, and nude photo.*

Sumner had a construction job and was doing quite well until he began flirting with a big, husky riveter. "Get away from me, you fag," roared the giant, "or I'll give you this jackhammer up your rear!"

Sumner bent over and said, "A promise is a promise!"

*　　*　　*

What would you call a toilet paper salesman on Fire Island?

Mary, Queen of Scotts.

*　　*　　*

On a men's room wall was written:
*My mother made me a homosexual.*
Right below it someone wrote:
*If I buy her the yarn will she make me one, too?*

*　　*　　*

Sylvester went to church and put a $20 bill in the collection plate. The minister said, "If the kind soul who donated the $20 bill will stand up, I will allow him to pick the next hymn."

Sylvester stood up and said, "Okay. I'll pick him, and him, and him!"

Hear about the most famous interior decorator in Wisconsin?

The queer that made Milwaukee famous.

\* \* \*

## PANSY

*One who likes his vice versa*

\* \* \*

Gaylord and Simon were sitting in the last row of a theater watching a horror movie.

"Ain't it gruesome?" asked Gaylord.

"It sure has!" said Simon.

\* \* \*

*There once was a queer named Broom*
*Who invited a guy to his room.*
   *They argued all night*
   *As to who had the right*
*To do what, with which and to whom.*

\* \* \*

Have you heard about the perverted Aussie who left his wife and went back to Sydney?

Did you hear about the new head of the Mafia in Miami?

He's a queer. From now on the *Kiss of Death* includes dinner and dancing.

\* \* \*

Holding a butterfly in his palm, Basil walked into a cocktail lounge. "See this butterfly?" he shouted. "If somebody will tell me how much this butterfly weighs, I'll bestow all my charm on him."

"Shut up, you bum," shouted a man at the bar. "It weighs a hundred pounds."

"Oh, sweetheart, you win!"

\* \* \*

The real estate agent phoned his employment service and said, "I fired the last three secretaries you sent over. Your first girl sang at her desk, the second was a vicious gossip, and this last chick was constantly popping her bubble gum. Now I want you to hire me a pansy . . . at least he won't open his mouth unless he means business."

\* \* \*

Did you hear about the gay guy who was so ugly he had to go out with girls?

# CHIMPANZEE

*A gay monkey*

*   *   *

A burly truck driver sauntered into a tavern in a mean mood, obviously looking for a fight.

"Everybody on this side of the bar is a no-good dirty bum!" he shouted. "Anybody want to make something of it—just stand up!"

Nobody stood up.

"Everybody on this side of the bar is a faggot! A fairy!"

No one moved. Then suddenly a man stood up.

"You wanna fight?" snarled the truck driver.

"No," lisped the man, "it's just that I'm on the wrong side of the bar."

*   *   *

*Doctor:* There's no need to worry. The next time you're troubled with insomnia, simply count sheep.

*Casper:* If it's all the same to you, Doctor, I'd rather count rams.

Did you hear about the two lavender lads who jumped on a bus and shouted, "Leave the driver to us"?

* * *

The psychiatrist was telling his patient, "It took us three years, but now you are cured. This is your last treatment."

"Thanks, Doc," said his patient. "But before I leave, kiss me."

"I tell you that you're all cured. You are a healthy person again."

"I know, Doc, but kiss me."

"You don't understand. I got rid of all those crazy ideas. You're cured."

"Sure," his patient persisted, "but just kiss me."

"Kiss you? I shouldn't even be on the couch with you!"

* * *

## GAY BLADE

*The Fire Island Fencing Champion*

* * *

Did you hear about the pair of hip parents who had their baby christened in Greenwich Village so the little one could have a fairy godfather?

Then there was the gay fellow who re-decorated his bathroom with His and His towels.

*     *     *

# LATENT HOMOSEXUALITY

*Swishful Thinking*

*     *     *

"They wouldn't have caught me," simpered the gay cadet at the military college, "if I hadn't tried to switch majors."

*     *     *

Two handsome hairdressers were sitting in a swish bar. "How about getting together tonight?" asked the first.

"I can't," answered the other. "I just came from the dentist and my mouth is all swollen!"

*     *     *

One day, back when the draft was still in effect, Glascox received his induction notice. He reported to his draft board and confessed that he was a homosexual.

"Queer, huh?" one member grunted. "Do you think you could kill a man?"

"Oh, yes," giggled Glascox, "but it would take me quite a while."

39

Dennis, on his first trip to New York, was being shown the sights by his friend Conrad.

One day they were out for a walk and were crossing the Verrazano Bridge. "Oh, just look at those great big boats," exclaimed Dennis. "Aren't they just simply beautiful?"

"They sure are," replied Conrad, "and such great big things."

"Lookie over there!" exclaimed Dennis. "That one's different from all the rest. Whatever kind of a boat can that be?"

"You big silly," explained Conrad, "that's a ferry boat."

"Oh, mercy," said Dennis, "I knew we were strong, but I didn't know we had a Navy!"

\* \* \*

## PHAGOCYTE

*A gay gathering place*

\* \* \*

What is the difference between a choir boy and a queer boy?

The difference is in how they say A-men.

Members of this group wishing to take female hormones shall report to classes in *artificial infemination.*

\* \* \*

During World War II the draft board examiners eyed the swishy young man with suspicion. They had orders to watch out for potential draft evaders feigning homosexuality. After subjecting the chap to an extensive physical and psychological examination, one of the board members declared, "Well, fella, it looks to me like you're going to make a good little soldier."

"Fabulous!" replied the young man. "When do I meet him?"

\* \* \*

> Said Jane to her mother, "I fear
> My husband's turned into a queer.
>    On Sundays and Mondays
>    He irons my undies,
> And he secretly wears my brassiere.

\* \* \*

Did you hear about the gay Manhattanite who moved to Long Island so he could be listed in the Queens directory?

A man vacationing at a nudist camp for the first time was surprised to see a large sign at the edge of the woods that read: BEWARE OF HOMOSEXUALS!

A little way into the woods, he came across another sign, and then another, and then a whole series of them, each slightly smaller and lower than the last, but all with the same wording: BEWARE OF HOMOSEXUALS!

Finally, he came upon a very small sign and he had to bend way over to make it out.

It read: WE WARNED YOU!

# GAY DECEIVER

*A dyke in drag*

\* \* \*

"But Mom, all the girls my age are wearing training bras."

"Shut up, Stanley. You're lucky I bought you the garter belt."

\* \* \*

The wife of a well-known film producer was entertaining a number of guests one evening. During one point of the party her ten-year-old son flitted into the room, arrayed in a strapless black evening gown, his lips covered with lipstick, high-heeled suede shoes on his feet, and a feathered hat on his head. Quite naturally, the woman was stunned.

"Rodney!" she cried. "You naughty, naughty boy! Go upstairs and remove your father's clothes before he comes in and catches you!"

\* \* \*

## HEADLINE IN GREENWICH VILLAGE PAPER

*Hurricane Bruce Has Struck Fire Island*

A Lesbian approached a beautiful blonde at a cocktail party. "Baby," cooed the dyke, "I could make some heavenly music with you."

"Yeah?" snapped the blonde. "Not without a baton, you couldn't!"

* * *

## TRANSVESTITE

*A sham ma'am*

* * *

The bartender was explaining to the sergeant in charge of the Riot Squad, "I can't imagine what started the brawl. A bunch of Dutch immigrants had just come into the bar, and one of them was telling everyone how some kid back home got to be a big hero by poking his finger in a dyke. All of a sudden, the tough-looking dame came up and punched him in the mouth. What for, I don't know."

* * *

Gina and Gertrude, sporting butch haircuts, were sitting at a "ladies" bar.

"Do you know that people get leprosy from having heterosexual relations?"

"Really?" said Gertrude.

"Not really, but *spread* the rumor!"

45

# LESBIANS

*Bosom buddies*

\* \* \*

To cut down on expenses, two secretaries decided to vacation together and to share a hotel room. On the first night, one turned to her friend and rested her hand on her shoulder.

"There's something about myself I've never told you," she admitted. "I'll be frank..."

"No," said the other girl, "I'll be Frank."

\* \* \*

# LIBERATED LADIES

*Licentious Lawyers * Libidinous
Librarians * Lecherous Lumberjills *
Lascivious Laundresses * Lustful
Legislators * Luscious Lickety-
Splits*

\*     \*     \*

*Bartender:*  What's your pleasure?
*Blonde:*  Balling, but I guess I'll have a martini.

        *     *     *

The gynecologist completed his examination. "I'm sorry, miss," he said, "but removal of that vibrator is going to involve a very delicate operation!"

"I'm not sure I can afford it, Doc," sighed the girl. "Why don't you just replace the batteries?"

When they finally got to her pad, Connie asked bachelor Blake, "You're not one of those guys who goes in for weird kicks, are you?"

"Not me!" grinned Blake. "I'd have to be stone drunk to ask you to do anything kinky."

"The liquor's under the sink," said Connie.

Grant and his girl were standing together in a nudist colony. "When I say I love you," he asked, "why do you lower your eyes?"

"To see if it's true!" she replied.

\* \* \*

## OVERHEARD AT A SINGLES BAR

"I'm a home-loving girl," she declared. "Shall we go to my home or yours?"

\* \* \*

Felix was fussing at his girlfriend. "I don't mind people saying that I'm playing second fiddle, but when they say I'm playing third and fourth fiddle . . . I can't take it!"

She just laughed and said, "With a slip horn as small as yours you're lucky to be in the orchestra!"

\* \* \*

*A frank female rebel named Glutz*
*Disdained any ifs, ands, or buts;*
*When they asked what she'd need*
*To be totally freed*
*Of her hang-up, her answer was "Nuts!"*

Otis flipped over Gloria. There was nothing in life he wanted more than to possess her, body and soul.

"Gloria," he pleaded, "I'll do anything to prove my love for you—just name it. I'll give you anything you want—furs, jewels, a castle in Spain. All I want is to make you happy. Test me and I'll prove my only wish is to please you."

Gloria looked at him and said, "Okay, Otis, I'd like to make it with your friend Herb."

\* \* \*

*He:* Do you like to make it with the lights on or off?

*She:* Yes.

\* \* \*

At a Park Avenue cocktail party, stunning Steve had his eye on a delicious blonde for an hour. He finally sidled up to her. "If I give you $50, will you sleep with me?"

"Sure," she replied. "But if we don't sleep, it's gonna cost you another hundred!"

*Three gals and a coxswain named Jensen*
*Were marooned on the Isle of Ascension,*
　*The ladies got tough*
　*And swam off in a huff:*
*The man was the bone of contention!*

\* \* \*

While Ryan was struggling with a jammed cigarette machine in the lobby of a Detroit hotel, his hand slipped off the knob and his elbow struck a passing girl on the chest.

"I'm terribly sorry," said Ryan. "But if your heart is as soft as your breast, you'll forgive me."

"Oh, I do," she answered, smiling, "And if the rest of you is as hard as your elbow, my room is 912!"

\* \* \*

Margaret walked up to the bowlegged druggist and asked, "May I have some talcum powder, please?"

"Yes, ma'am," he said, "walk right this way."

"If I could walk that way," she replied, "I wouldn't need any talcum powder."

* * *

A subway train was stuck for over an hour. The lights were out and it was pitch black. A woman turned to the man standing beside her and said, "Look, mister, either stop talking about your wife or take your hand off my ass!"

* * *

*1st Steno:* Hasn't he got a handsome profile?

*2nd Steno:* You mean halfway down? That's no profile, take my word for it. Those are his keys.

* * *

"I can't understand it, Doctor," complained Helen. "Every time I see a handsome, muscular man on the beach, I get this funny feeling between my toes."

"That's strange," said the medico. "Which toes?"

"The big ones," she sighed.

Grace lay on the psychiatrist's couch.

"Close your eyes and relax," said the shrink, "and I'll try an experiment." He took a leather key case from his pocket, flipped it open, and shook the keys. "What did that sound remind. you of?" he asked.

"Sex," she whispered.

Then he closed the key case and touched it to the girl's upturned palm. Her body stiffened.

"And that?" asked the psychiatrist.

"Sex," Grace murmured nervously.

"Now open your eyes," instructed the doctor, "and tell me why what I did was sexually evocative to you."

Hesitantly, her eyelids flickered open. Grace saw the key case in the psychiatrist's hand and blushed scarlet. "Well—er—to begin with," she stammered, "I thought that first sound was your zipper opening . . ."

"*I thought I heard your zipper opening!*"

Harold started hitchhiking and in just a few moments he was picked up by Eleanor, a lucious-looking librarian. "Would you like a cigarette?" he asked.

"No, thanks," she replied. "I don't smoke!"

They rode in silence for a short time and Harold said, "I know a nice bar up the road here, would you like to stop and have a drink?"

"Thank you, no," said Eleanor. "I don't drink!"

Ten minutes later, Harold took a wild shot and said, "Why don't we stop at the next motel and make love?"

She said, "All right!"

They stopped, made it like mad for two solid hours, and then were back driving in her car.

"Say, I'm curious," said Harold. "When I asked you to have a smoke, you said no. When I offered to buy you a drink, you turned me down. Yet you went to the motel with me. How come?"

"Well," said the librarian, "I always practice what I preach. I tell my Sunday school class that you don't have to smoke or drink to have a good time!"

\*   \*   \*

*1st Secretary:*   Did you enjoy the cocktail party you went to last night?

*2nd Secretary:* Enjoy it? One more drink and I'd have been under the host.

\* \* \*

Did you hear about the female activist who went berserk during a demonstration and attacked a karate-trained cop with a deadly weapon?

She ended up a chopped libber.

\* \* \*

Two emancipated young chicks were out driving on a highway when it began raining.

"Never mind the rain," said the girl beside the driver, "put on some speed."

"No, the cops might catch us!" said her friend, "and we can't be fixing any tickets with the grass this wet!"

\* \* \*

*A mortician's sly daughter named*
*    Maddie*
*Told an eager but virginal laddie,*
*  "If you'll do as I say,*
*  We can have a great lay,*
*Since I've buried more stiffs than my*
*    daddy."*

Ted met Karen, a pretty young lawyer, at a cocktail party and their relationship grew warmer as the party progressed.

"Sweetheart," he finally said to her, "it's almost midnight—why don't we end this with a kiss?"

"If you really want to," replied the attorney. "Personally, I'd rather go to your place and finish it with a bang."

\* \* \*

First Divorcée: How did you get your divorce?
Second Divorcée: It wasn't hard.

\* \* \*

Collins became quite upset when he learned that Milly, his nineteen-year-old daughter, had hitchhiked alone from Seattle to San Diego.

"Why, you could have been molested, assaulted—raped!" he stormed.

"I was perfectly safe, Dad," said Milly. "Every time a man picked me up, I explained that I was going to San Diego because it has the best VD clinic on the Coast."

Larson took Charlotte for a drive way out in the country and parked the car in a desolate stretch. "If you try to molest me," said Charlotte, "I'll scream!"

"What good would that do?" asked Larson. "There isn't a soul around for miles."

"I know," said Charlotte, "but I want to satisfy my conscience before I start having a good time."

\* \* \*

A sailor met a gal at a dance hall. It got to be around 11 o'clock. "Aren't you gonna take me home?" asked the girl.

"Is there anything in it?" said the sailor.

"Just a little dust from dancing!"

\* \* \*

Boy: I'm tired of this fooling around. I'm coming over to your apartment tonight and I'm going to throw you down on the couch and pull off your pants . . .

Girl: Oh, no, you're not!

Boy: And I'm going to screw you so hard you won't be able to walk straight!

Girl: Oh, no, you're not!

Boy: And what's more, I'm not even going to wear a condom.

Girl: Oh, yes, you are!

\* \* \*

# WOMEN'S LIB LAMENT

*Human reproduction is a regressive process: It begins with coming to the point and ends with straddling the issue.*

\* \* \*

Mrs. Middleton was talking to the family doctor. "It's silly," she said, "but my daughter has some sort of crazy idea to lose her hair."

"How so?" asked the medical man.

"Well, I overheard her on the phone the other day telling her closest friend that she hoped she'd be bald soon."

\* \* \*

*John:* If you'll give me a kiss, it'll be a feather in my cap.

*Jane:* Stick around! I'll make you an Indian chief!

\* \* \*

Marie walked into the office. "My, but you look different!" said one of her co-workers. "Your hair is extra curly and you have a sort of wide-eyed look. What did you use—special curlers and some dramatic new eye makeup?"

"No," said Marie. "My vibrator shorted out this morning."

*   *   *

"I believe in love at first sight," confided the girl to her roommate. "The first time I saw one, I just knew I'd love it."

*   *   *

The shapely new stenographer gave a piece of paper to the company auditor, saying, "Here's that report you wanted, Mr. Berry!"

"My name is Mr. Perry!" he corrected. "You must have been talking to the head bookkeeper who can't pronounce his P's right. Did he say anything about me?"

"Only that when it comes to meaningless details, you're a regular brick!"

*   *   *

"And do you perform fellatio?" asked the intrusive sex pollster.

"It all depends," replied the girl, "on the fella."

Marion was a wealthy, middle-aged matron in great physical need. Tom was in his healthy twenties. They met at a cocktail party and Marion brought Tom home to her apartment.

As they headed for the bedroom, Marion said, "Tomorrow, I'll send you a little present. If you're really good, you'll get a Cadillac. If you're only fair, it'll be a Pontiac. If you're just so-so, you'll get a Volkswagen!"

Four hours later, Tom got dressed and prepared to leave. "Well," he asked, "how was I?"

"You'll know in the morning," she replied, "when the mailman delivers the pair of roller skates!"

\* \* \*

How times have changed!

The old-fashioned girl used to take a couple of drinks and go out like a light.

Today the liberated lady takes a couple of drinks—and out goes the light.

\* \* \*

*Day Nurse:*    Did you notice the man in Room 218 with the word SWAN tattooed on his penis?

64

*Night Nurse:*  That's not SWAN—it's
SASKATCHEWAN!

\* \* \*

Ozzie got himself a new girlfriend
whom he entertained at every opportunity,
in her apartment.

One day she remarked, "Ozzie, you must
have been an army man."

"That's right," he said. "Artillery. How
did you know?"

"Because," replied she, "you always like
to end the evening with a bang!"

\* \* \*

*There was a young lady from Plain
    View
Whose boyfriend said, "May I explore
    you?
  She replied to the chap,
  "I will draw you a map
Where others have been to before
    you."*

\* \* \*

*Customer:*  How much will you take off for
cash?
*Salesgirl:*  Sir! . . . Er, how much cash?

The booth at the benefit bazaar bore a sign that said: KISSES: $1 TO $25.

A prospective customer walked up to the beautiful model in attendance. "Is the range in price a matter of duration?" he asked. "Or perhaps of lip pressure?"

"No," smiled the beauty. "Lip *placement!*"

*"It's where you place your lips!"*

*There was a young miss from*
    *Dumfries*
*Who said to her date, "If you please,*
    *It would give me great bliss*
    *If, while fondling this,*
*You would pay some attention to*
    *these."*

\*     \*     \*

Josh, a wealthy stockbroker, was crazy about Erica, a beautiful redhead. Unfortunately, he wasn't getting to first base, so he decided the only way he could have her was to marry her.

On their next date, after a champagne in his apartment, he said, "Darling, will you be my wife? I have enough money to get you anything your heart desires."

"No, Josh, you can't buy my love," replied Erica. "However, if the price is right I might possibly *rent* you some."

\*     \*     \*

## SIGN IN A STORE WINDOW

*Male Help Wanted!*
*An opening for an up-and-coming young man with lots of push to fill vacancy left by death of owner's husband.*
*Apply within.*

The nymphomaniac was calling collect. "Would you repeat the name, please!" said the telephone operator.

"Yes, Alice. ALICE! A as in Adultery. L as in Lust. I as in Incest. C as in Copulation. E as in Erotic. . . ."

\* \* \*

Diedra and Marni grew up together and were real swingers. They swung through their teens and 20s and 30s, even their 40s and 50s. The girls got married and still they continued to make it with everybody, everywhere, and in every place.

Then Diedra's husband died. Two years later, Diedra passed away. At her bier friends were in line saying their last goodbyes. When Marni got to the coffin she began wailing, "At last! At last they're together!"

A woman hearing her cries said, "What do you mean, 'at last they're together'? She was the biggest swinger who ever lived."

"At last," shouted Marni, "at last her legs are together!"

\* \* \*

Marge: I had a date with two guys last night.

Diane: Really? How'd you manage to fit them both in?

"No, I will not go to the movies with you!" said Jackie. "I know your kind! As soon as we're seated, you'll start fiddling with my blouse buttons with one hand and tugging at my skirt with the other, getting ready to take liberties!"

"No, I wouldn't," protested Patrick. "The people sitting behind us could see what I was up to."

"Yes, that's true," said Jackie, "so maybe we'd better get there early and find seats in the last row."

\* \* \*

A cute little chick from Chattanooga was cruising down the highway when she spotted a handsome young stud hitchhiking. She braked her sports car to a stop and invited him to get in.

An hour later, she said, "You'd better get off here, this is as far as I go."

So he got off her and she started up her car and drove on.

\* \* \*

*Shiela:* (from bedroom) Has the milkman come yet?

*Roommate:* (from kitchen) No, but he's breathing hard!

"What," Gwen asked her date, "is hot-blooded, passionate, and hums?"

The young man thought a bit, and answered, "I don't know."

Gwen smiled and replied, "Hmmm . . ."

\* \* \*

The stunningly stacked babe appeared at her door in a strapless evening gown that defied gravity.

"Groovy!" said her admiring escort. "I don't see what holds that dress up!"

"Play your cards right," she murmured, "and you might."

\* \* \*

A muscle-bound beach bum was showing off by lifting two bikinied beauties high in the air, one on each arm. "Wow," said a nearby girl-watcher to his crony, "look at the dolls on that boob!"

\* \* \*

"Let's make this a Dutch treat," suggested the cute receptionist. "If you pay for the dinner and the nightclub, the rest of the night can be on me!"

The young man had offered Harriet a ride home after work. He was entertaining and handsome, so she invited him up for a drink.

One thing led to another, and they spent a wonderful night together. But when Harriet woke up, her companion had already dressed and left, and she realized that she knew little about him except his first name.

Determined not to lose this real find, she remembered that he had said that he worked on a game-bird farm. Harriet telephoned the place, gave his first name and described him.

"Yeah," said the man on the phone, "that's Pete Morrell, lady. He's a pheasant plucker."

"He sure is!" agreed the girl. "And he has a pleasant smile and personality, too."

\* \* \*

Sitting in a hotel lobby, Oscar spotted a lovely looking lady passing through. He siddled up to her and said, "Hi there, beautiful!"

Her stare froze him in his tracks.

"Sorry," said Oscar, "I thought you were my mother!"

"I couldn't be," she snapped. "I'm married."

\* \* \*

They met on Friday night at a singles bar. After several minutes of chit-chat she asked, "What are your plans for the rest of the evening?"

"I'm gonna find me a hot chick," he answered. "I'm gonna ask her up to my pad, mix her a few drinks, put her on the couch, turn out the lights, and make mad, passionate love to her. What do you think of that?"

She smiled. "It sounds like a great idea, if you ask me!"

\* \* \*

1st Secretary: What's the difference between a paper clip and a screw?

2nd Secretary: I don't know! I've never been paper clipped.

"Where'd you get the mink?" asked Cheryl.

"Oh," answered Madge. "This real smooth executive type picked me up in a cocktail lounge, took me to dinner and a show, and then we went to his apartment. After we'd had some Courvoisier he opened a huge closet, and there were a bunch of full-length minks, and he said, 'Pick one out.'"

"And you didn't have to do anything?" asked Cheryl.

"Well," said Madge, "naturally, I had to take it up about six inches."

*"I had to take it up about six inches!"*

Janet, a pert secretary, sashayed into the boss' office. "I have some good news and some bad news," she announced.

"No jokes please," said her boss, "not on quarterly report day. Just give me the good news."

"Okay," declared the girl. "The good news is that you're not sterile."

* * *

*There is a young trollop named Mabel*
*Who's ready and willing and able.*
*And so kind she'd not think*
*To ask rubies or mink*
*Which is why she wears diamonds*
*and sable.*

* * *

*Lorraine:* I've got an awful headache!
*Lois:* When I have a headache my husband soothes all the pain away; all he has to do is to rub the back of my neck then caress my forehead lightly, then plant a little kiss on my mouth and before you know it the headache is gone! Why don't you try it?
*Lorraine:* I think I will. When does your husband get home?

Convicted of murder and sentenced to death, the shapely young lady asked, as a last request, that she be hanged in the nude.

Although the warden thought this unusual, he felt a last request was not something to be denied. When the condemned prisoner arrived at the gallows the hangman gasped, "My God, you have the most beautiful body I've ever seen."

Came the whispered reply, "It's all yours if you keep your trap shut."

\* \* \*

The old-fashioned girl who used to cry, "Stop, or I'll scream," now has a daughter who yells, "Hurry up or I'll scream!"

\* \* \*

The god Thor was bored drinking mead in Valhalla and came down to earth. He met a chorus girl in Las Vegas and they went to bed and stayed there for three days and nights. On leaving the fourth morning, he decided to tell her how signally she had been honored.

"My dear," he said, "I'm Thor!"

"You're Thor?" she exclaimed. "I'm tho thore I can't even pith!"

Francine was inclined to talk just a little too much about her ability to stimulate men. "Just think," she burbled to the office in general one morning, "a wealthy gentleman from Texas took me out last evening! He told me several times how much he valued my company, and then, when he said good night—as a small token of his esteem—he slipped two 100-dollar bills into my purse!"

"Well, well," came a female voice from the other side of the file cabinets, "that's the first time I've ever heard of a 180-dollar tip."

\* \* \*

# HAPPY HOOKERS

*High-Class Hussies * Hopped-Up
Harridans * Soft-Hearted Harlots *
Cat-House Harlequins * Horny
Hustlers * Hanky Panky Procurers*

\*    \*    \*

Kenneth stopped a Times Square street-walker and asked, "Do you honor credit cards?"

"Honey," replied the prostie, "I not only honor, I love and obey them!"

\* \* \*

Lloyd went to visit his favorite lady of the evening. He rang the bell and found there was no answer. Then, he put on his glasses and read a note that was pinned to the door:

ON VACATION.  DO IT YOURSELF.

She snuggled up to him and whispered, "I'm yours for the asking . . . I'm asking fifty dollars."

* * *

# PROSTITUTE

*A busy body*

* * *

"That was the best loving of my life!" exclaimed the yokel. "I only wish I had something to remember you by."

"That can be fixed!" yawned the prostie. "Stop off downstairs, and the madam will write you out a receipt."

* * *

The doorbell rang at Polly's Peace Emporium. As Polly started toward the door, one of the girls happened to glance out the window. "Don't open it, Madame!" she cried.

"Why?" asked Polly. "Is it the fuzz?"

"N-n-no, ma'am, it's just one fellow ringing the bell," stammered the harlot, "but he's standing way out in the street!"

Sherry slammed the bedroom door and stormed into the madam's office.

"Don't be upset, honey," soothed the madam. "How does he want it? Against the wall? In the bathtub? On the carpet? Bottoms up?"

"No," replied Sherry, "he runs the popcorn stand on the corner, and he wants it for peanuts!"

*　*　*

*Madame:* Mona, just how accomplished are you?

*Mona:* I don't like to brag, but I can make love standing on my head!

*Madame:* Then you're the one I want . . . there's a yogi waiting downstairs.

*　*　*

"I've been getting a lot of complaints from clients about you," said the madame to one of her girls.

"Listen," snapped the prostitute, "I give my johns as good a time as any other girl in the place!"

"Maybe you do in most ways," the madame retorted, "but there's just this one thing—stop whistling while you work!"

83

# MADAME

*One for whom the belles toil*

\*    \*    \*

Balkin, a Chicago manufacturer, was squiring a big buyer around town. They went to the best restaurant and had a fine dinner. "Enjoy it?" asked Balkin.

"Not bad," answered the customer, "but where're the girls?"

Balkin quickly checked his black book, made a phone call, and soon the two were on their way uptown. At their destination, they entered a reception room where they found several attractive girls. One old enough to be their mother approached them.

"Are you boys married or single?" asked the madame.

"What the hell is the difference?" bellowed Balkin.

"Because," said the madame, "we take care of the needy, not the greedy."

\*    \*    \*

A mortuary opened up across the street from Belle's place. In a few days, the mortician installed an enormous neon sign reading:

## OUR STAFF WILL STUFF
## YOUR STIFF

Belle, very proud of her house, wasn't about to have some mortuary "outdo" her with a great big sign. Two weeks later, the mortician was shocked to see a newly installed sign on the whorehouse roof:

## OUR STUFF WILL STIFF
## YOUR STAFF

\* \* \*

*There was a young harlot from Kew*
*Who filled her inside up with glue.*
*She said with a grin*
*"If they pay to get in*
*They'll pay to get out of it, too."*

\* \* \*

Call girl Clemina was a legend in her own time. When she quit the profession, the telephone company retired her number.

\* \* \*

## SIGN IN A HOUSE OF
## PROSTITUTION

*No cash*
*No gash!*

85

Benson went to a bordello and was surprised to see the unshaven armpits of the hooker as she undressed.

"So much wool, so much wool!" he muttered. As she slipped out of her undies, he caught sight of another prodigious growth.

"So much wool, so much wool!" said Benson again.

"Look fella," snapped the girl, "did you come here to get laid, or to knit?"

In Manhattan, you can now purchase a call-girl directory. It's called *Who's Whore*.

*    *    *

Schroeder walked into a house of ill repute and requested a woman. "Sorry," said the madame, "all the girls are taken for the night. But we've got a guy here named Schmitz who's unique. Try him. If he doesn't make you happy, I'll give you back your money."

Schroeder tried Schmitz and left very pleased. He returned the next night and asked for Schmitz. "He's off tonight," said the madame. "How about the guy who's filling in for Schmitz?"

"No, thanks," said the man. "Far as I'm concerned, if you're out of Schmitz, you're out of queer!"

*    *    *

## MAKE SHIFT

*A call girl's gown*

*    *    *

Upon entering the taxi and noticing the driver was a woman, Donald decided to have a little fun. "Miss," he said, "take me to the cheapest brothel in town."

"Mister," replied the female cabbie, "you're in it!"

* * *

*A shapely young lady named Fern*
*Puts out and is paid in return*
  *"And my earnings," she said*
  *"I conceal in my bed,*
*Since the ads say to save where you*
    *earn."*

* * *

Wally went to a whorehouse and said to the madame, "I want a girl with big boobs and a small box!"

"Why?" she asked.

"Never mind!" replied Wally, "I'm paying for it. I want a girl with big tits and a small cooze!"

"Okay," said the madame, "go up to room 3."

Five minutes later there was a knock on the door of Wally's room. A girl walked in.

"Okay," she said, "are you the guy with the big mouth and the small pecker?"

# PIMP

*A fornicaterer*

\* \* \*

Jerome, in Cleveland on business, picked up a lovely chick in the hotel bar and took her up to his room. After a few drinks, the girl sat on his lap.

"Would you like to hug me?" she cooed.

"Sure," said Jerome, pulling her close.

"And would you like to kiss me?" asked the girl.

"Of course," replied Jerome, planting a long kiss on her lips.

"Okay, honey," she continued, "brace yourself—because here comes the 50-dollar question."

\* \* \*

Bonnie was recently investigated by the IRS. She listed her apartment rent as "expenses incurred while entertaining clients."

\* \* \*

# CALL GIRL

*A negotiable blonde*

Roger, the handsome real estate agent, couldn't remember when he'd rented an apartment to a more desirable tenant. As she bent over his desk to sign the lease, he became aware that his pulse was beating in his ears with the sound of bongo drums.

"Well," he said, "that's that. I wish you much happiness in your new apartment, and here are the two keys that come with it."

She straightened up, accepted the keys, and favored him with a dazzling smile. "And here's a month's rent in advance, honey," she replied. And she handed him back one of the keys.

\* \* \*

## PIMP

*A snatch purser*

\* \* \*

Flora met Dodi on Park Avenue. "Honey," said Flora, "would you please lend me ten dollars until I get back on my back?"

\* \* \*

Did you hear about the call girl who got tired of spending all her time in bed—so she settled for a desk job?

Doris, Carol, and Marla were arrested and brought into night court. The judge looked at Doris and she rolled her eyes and exhibited her legs. "What's your business?" the judge demanded.

"Well, Judge," she cooed. "I'm a dressmaker, and this awful cop . . ."

"Thirty days," interrupted his honor.

Carol was called and she tried the weeping stunt. "Oh, your Honor, I'm a respectable dressmaker with a family to support, a crippled mother, and a dying baby . . ."

"Thirty days," rasped the judge.

Marla was called to order and the judge asked, "What's your business?"

"I'm a whore," she answered.

"How's business?" he asked.

"Just lousy," said Marla, "what with all these dressmakers around."

*"The dressmakers are killing the business."*

A group of 100 freshmen from an up-state college each contributed $2 to the kitty. When the money was collected, they drew lots to see which one would visit Violet, the town's call girl, who charged $200 a visit.

That night, the winner, pimply-faced Horace, went to Violet's apartment and handed her the money.

"That's a lot of money for a college boy to have," said Violet. Horace explained how each guy had put up two dollars and had drawn lots to see who would enjoy her favors.

She was touched by the story. "I'm going to do something that I've never done before," said Violet. "I'm going to give you back your money."

Then she gave him back his two dollars.

\* \* \*

## SIGN IN A MONTREAL SUBWAY

*Stop screwing around—patronize your local brothel!*

\* \* \*

Noreen, aged twenty, stood before the magistrate as the arresting officer read off her record. It seemed she had spent most of her teen years in jail or on bail for pursuing the oldest of professions.

"How on earth did you ever get started in this life?" asked the judge. "At what age did you first begin this practice?"

"Your Honor," said Noreen, "when I was about ten years old a little boy my age told me that's what little girls were for. And do you know, Judge, of all the grown up men I have met since then, not a damn one has ever told me different!"

\*   \*   \*

Did you hear about the former farm girl now living on Park Avenue who says she gets a grand and glorious feeling whenever a man makes love to her?

But the grand always comes first.

\*   \*   \*

Calvin picked up a Park Avenue hooker and made it with her standing up in an alley. She kept nodding everytime he thrust.

"You like it, eh?" he asked.

"Yes," she nodded vigorously. "But you've got a bit of my scarf tucked in."

95

Muriel and Tina were discussing their recent experiences over cocktails.

"Say," asked Muriel, "how did you make out with that eccentric millionaire you met yesterday?"

"He gave me $500," said Tina. "That screwball wanted to make it in a coffin."

"No kidding!" exclaimed Muriel. "I'll bet that shook you up?"

"Yeah, but not as much as the six pallbearers."

*A clever commercial female*
*Had prices tatooed on her tail.*
*And on her behind*
*For the sake of the blind*
*Was the same information in Braille.*

\* \* \*

Oscar and Justin, two car salesmen, were seated at a bar comparing notes over martinis.

"Boy, if I don't get out of here and sell some cars," exclaimed Oscar, "I'm going to lose my ass this month!"

Too late he realized a beautiful blonde sitting two stools down had overheard him.

"I'm sorry, miss!" said Oscar.

"Forget it," she replied, "I know how you feel. If I don't get rid of some ass this month, I'm going to lose my car!"

\* \* \*

"I'm through going to psychiatrists," cried the call girl. "I just can't get used to a guy who tells me to lie down on a couch and then sends me a bill."

\* \* \*

## OFFSPRING OF A PROSTITUTE

*Brothel sprouts*

Did you hear about the whore in the leper colony?

She did all right till her business dropped off.

* * *

One day, Mrs. Robert Milbank bumped into her old hooker mate, Florence, on Fifth Avenue.

"Gee, Flo," she said, "I haven't seen you for a dog's age. Where've you been?"

"Oh," said the streetwalker, "I've been up here on Fifth Avenue for the last two years. You see, when my daughter Irene got married, I gave her Park Avenue for a wedding present."

* * *

Then there's this swinging call girl who's a pleasure to be with—but she doesn't come cheap.

* * *

"Darling," said the new bride, "I can't thank you enough for changing my name!"

"You mean from Harrison to Harrigan?" asked the groom.

"No," said the bride. "From hustler to housewife!"

Through a mix-up, Priscilla and Raymond, total strangers, held the same ticket for a compartment on a train going from New York to Los Angeles. There were no other available rooms, so they settled the argument by agreeing to share the compartment.

Raymond wined and dined Priscilla for three days and every night he pitched, but it was no go. He couldn't get to first base, and he never made out. All he got was more frustrated. Finally, on the last day, he asked her, "Why, what's wrong with me?"

"Honey, you're a nice fella," said Priscilla, "but I'm a New York hooker and I'm on vacation."

"*Sorry, but I'm on vacation!*"

What course does a prostitute take in college?

Whorticulture!

*　　*　　*

A switchman was accosted by a streetwalker down by the railroad yard. She convinced him to visit with her in a nearby shed. The railroad man, not too terribly enthusiastic, decided to use an iron rail spike instead of his pecker.

For ten minutes neither of the participants spoke. Then finally he asked, "Like it?"

"I'm sure glad you said something," answered the woman. "Your tool is so cold I was afraid you were dead!"

*　　*　　*

Have you heard about the 97-year-old prostitute who got herself listed in the Yellow Pages and now claims to be the oldest trick in the book?

*　　*　　*

Marty and his wife Louise sat at the bar of a Chicago hotel. Marty pointed to a striking blonde sitting at the other end and said, "That's a hooker."

"I don't believe it!" said Louise.

"I'll show you," said Marty.

He walked over and chatted with the blonde. Five minutes later, they were in his room.

"How much?" asked Marty.

"Fifty bucks."

"I'll give you twenty."

"Forget it!" said the prostie as she walked out the door.

A few minutes later, Marty rejoined his spouse at the bar. The call girl walked over and tapped him on the shoulder.

"You see," she said, "that's what you get for twenty dollars!"

\* \* \*

# SWINGING SPOUSES

*Shameful Shenanigans * Shocking*
*Shack-Ups * Sneaky Switching **
*Secret swapping * Scandalous*
*Screwing*

\* \* \*

The streetwalker tried to peddle her wares to a man on Park Avenue.

"I won't for three reasons," he replied. "I promised my wife, and I also promised my mother that I wouldn't fool around with strange women."

"What's your third excuse?" asked the prostie.

"I just had a piece!" he said.

\*   \*   \*

Wife:     You sure are a great lover, sugar.

Husband:  Thanks baby, there's nothing like a professional opinion!

*Nobody gave the bride away but several young men at the wedding could have.*

\* \* \*

"Honey," said the bride to the groom on their wedding night, "I have something to confess. I was once a topless dancer."

"Oh, no!" exclaimed the husband. "Not that! I honestly think I'd rather have married a girl who'd been a prostitute."

"You do? Well, there's another thing . . ."

\* \* \*

Benjy and Herman, a couple of slick studs, checked into a motel room and telephoned down for a call girl.

Ten minutes later she arrived by taxi and they both took turns in the adjoining room.

After they finished and the girl left, Benjy said, "She was okay, but I think my wife is better."

"Yeah," said Herman, "I have to agree; your wife is better."

\* \* \*

On a quiz show the emcee was interviewing a male contestant. "You say you met your wife at a brothel. Now, wasn't that romantic?"

"No, it was embarrassing," said the man. "I thought she was home tending the kids and she thought I was bowling. And to top it all, the madame refused to refund my money or give me another girl."

\* \* \*

*Brides should be well groomed on their honeymoon.*

\* \* \*

Willy had just returned from a week of honeymooning and his best friend asked him how it went.

"The first night we did it nine times," said Willy. "The second night, eight times. The third night, seven times. The fourth night, six times. The fifth night, five times. The sixth night, four times, and the last night, *nothing!*"

"Nothing?" asked his buddy. "How come?"

"Hey, you ever tried putting a marshmallow in a parking meter?"

The newlyweds stopped at a farmhouse and made a deal to bed down for the night. By noon the next day they were not up yet so the farmer yelled for them to come get some breakfast.

"No thanks," called the groom. "We're living on the fruits of love."

"Okay," screamed the farmer. "But quit throwing the damned skins out the window —they're choking the ducks!"

*　*　*

On the wedding morning the bride was very anxious to see Niagara Falls. The groom put up the window shade but it was raining.

They couldn't see the Falls, so they went back to bed. Same thing happened the second and third days. The fourth day the groom went to the window, took hold of the cord, and went up with the shade.

*　*　*

"Will I be the first to do this to you?" whispered the groom as he slipped into bed.

"What a silly question!" giggled the bride. "I don't even know what position you're going to use yet."

110

| | |
|---|---|
| *Expectant Father:* | This is my first baby. |
| *Old Hand:* | This is our seventh. |
| *Expectant Father:* | Well, gee, maybe you can answer a question for me. How soon after my wife has the baby can she and I, uh—you know what I mean. |
| *Old Hand:* | That depends on whether she's in a ward or a private room. |

\*   \*   \*

## IDEAL HUSBAND

*One who is well off and good on*

\*   \*   \*

Overheard in a Pullman traveling between Los Angeles and Chicago:

"I'm deeply sorry, ladies, I'm a married man, a man of respect and standing in my community. I cannot have a breath of scandal touch me. I am sorry, but . . . one of you girls will have to leave."

111

The groom went down to the hotel lobby to smoke a cigar while his bride was undressing, as she was too shy to undress while he was present.

When he came back up to their wedding suite he found her lying stark naked in bed on top of one bellboy who was copulating with her, while a second bellboy was playing with her boobs. She was holding a third bellboy, and two more were waiting their turn.

The bridegroom was thunderstruck.

"Madelaine!" he exclaimed. "How could you?"

"Oh, honey," she replied, "you know I've always been something of a flirt."

"*I've always been a bit of a flirt!*"

The husband and wife were having difficulty in deciding what to give up for Lent, but finally, in a fervent spirit of atonement, they agreed on sex.

As the weeks slowly passed, they began to regret their choice but still stuck to it, sleeping in separate bedrooms and also locking the doors to control temptation.

Finally, the glorious Easter sun rose, and the wife was awakened by a series of thunderous knocks on her door. "Oh, George," she called out, "I know what you're knocking for!"

"You're damn right!" he yelled back. "But do you know what I'm knocking *with?*"

\* \* \*

Wife, with hands cupped: "Guess what I've got in here and you can have a little piece tonight."

Husband, after a minute: "An elephant."

"That's close enough."

\* \* \*

Devlin asked the doctor to perform a vasectomy on him. "Well," asked the physician, "have you discussed the operation and its implications with your wife and family?"

"Yes," declared Devlin. "I'm sort of luke-warm about it myself, but my wife persuaded me to put it to a vote with the children."

"And what was the result?" asked the doctor.

"The kids favored it nine to four."

*　*　*

## SWINGING SPOUSES

*She runs after everything that wears pants, and he runs after everything that doesn't*

*　*　*

Two young suburban housewives who were both enthusiastic gardeners were discussing a new botanical theory.

"Do you really believe," asked one, "that talking affectionately to a plant can make it grow bigger?"

"I certainly do!" replied the other. "In my experience, anything organic can be increased in size by affectionate handling."

115

Sybil leaned across the bed, picked up the phone, and said, "Yes, dear," into it. "That's all right, don't hurry. Enjoy yourself. Goodbye."

When she hung up, the man lying beside her said, "Who was that?"

"My husband."

"What did he want?"

"He called to say he'd be home late tonight. He's downtown playing poker with you and a bunch of the boys."

\*　\*　\*

Did you hear about the boastful blonde who bragged that her husband had never found a stranger in her closet—they were all his friends!

\*　\*　\*

Blair came home an hour earlier than usual and found his wife stark naked in bed. When he asked why, she explained, "I'm protesting because I don't have anything to wear."

Blair pulled open the closet door. "That's ridiculous," he said. "Look in here. There's a yellow dress . . . a red dress . . . a print dress . . . a pants suit . . . *hi, Chris* . . . a green dress . . ."

Lars came home early one afternoon and found his wife lying naked on the bed, breathing heavily. "June, what's the matter?" he asked.

"I think I'm having a heart attack," she gasped.

Quickly, Lars rushed downstairs to phone a doctor when his son came rushing in and exclaimed, "Daddy! There's a naked man in the front closet!"

Lars opened the closet door and found his best friend cowering there. "For God's sake, Emil!" screamed Lars. "June is having a heart attack and here you are sneaking around scaring the children!"

\* \* \*

The outraged husband discovered his wife in bed with another man.

"What is the meaning of this?" he demanded. "Who is this fellow?"

"That seems like a fair question," said the wife, rolling over. "What *is* your name?"

\* \* \*

"Do you cheat on your wife?" asked the psychiatrist.

"Who else?" answered the patient.

117

Ellen and Dolph had been married thirty years and never missed a night of connubial bliss. One day Ellen visited her doctor and was told that she must have complete rest and quiet for six months or she would not live.

Ellen and Dolph decided they should stay completely apart during this period. She moved into an upstairs bedroom and he remained downstairs.

After three months of complete abstinence and solitude, his willpower collapsed, and Dolph started for her bedroom.

As he started to climb the stairs, he saw her coming down.

"Dear," she said, "I was just coming down to die."

"I'm glad, honey," he said, "because I was just going up to kill you."

"*I was coming up to kill you!*"

"I have to take every precaution to avoid pregnancy," confided the woman over the back fence.

"But hasn't your husband just had a vasectomy?" asked her neighbor.

"Yes—and that's why I have to take every precaution."

\* \* \*

"Young woman, why do you want to divorce your husband?" asked the marriage counselor.

"Incompatibility!"

"Now, now," he soothed, "just what is it that makes him incompatible?"

"He wakes up at two in the morning and wants to go home."

\* \* \*

"You beast! You animal!" cried the young cutie. "I'm going back to mother."

"Never mind," said the guy. "I'll go back to my wife."

As they were dressing to go out to dinner Ralph said to his spouse, "That sure is a beautiful necklace you're wearing."

"Yes, isn't it, darling?" replied his wife. "I found it in the back seat of your car."

*     *     *

Lacey walked into the police station and asked the desk sergeant if he could swear out a warrant for the arrest of the boarder living at his home.

"And what charge do you want placed against him?" queried the officer.

"Petty larceny," replied Lacey.

"All right. Now, just what do you mean by petty larceny?" asked the cop.

"Well," stammered Lacey, "it's this way. The boarder has been stealing my wife away from me—piece by piece!"

*     *     *

## SWINGING SUBURBAN HOUSEWIFE'S SONG

*There's as much difference between lovers and husbands as night and day*

Jerry was visiting his married friends Ethel and Richard.

"Rich, I can't help it," said Jerry. "Ethel turns me on something fierce. If I could pinch her on her backside just once, I'd give five thousand dollars!"

"For that kind of money," said Richard, "I don't think Ethel would mind. Go ahead, pinch her."

Ethel leaned over a chair and exposed her behind. Jerry looked long and hard. Finally, after about five minutes, he said, "I just can't do it."

"Why not," asked Richard, "haven't you got the nerve?"

"No, I haven't got the money."

*"I ain't got the money!"*

Mrs. Brent, a wealthy Beverly Hills socialite, was almost in tears. "Oh, Maria," she said to her Mexican maid. "I believe my husband is having an affair with his secretary."

"I don't believe it," snapepd Maria. "You're just saying that to make me jealous."

\* \* \*

*In olden times people who committed adultery were stoned; today, it's often the other way around.*

\* \* \*

"Good morning, ma'am, I've come to read the meter," the gas man said to a lady who had opened the door wearing only panties.

"How do I know that?" replied the bare-breasted babe. "How do I know you're not an uncontrollable sex maniac, come to take advantage of some poor defenseless housewife, who's alone in her house . . . and will be until 5:25 this evening?"

\* \* \*

Did you hear about the guy who never worried about his marriage, until he moved from New York to California and discovered he still had the same milkman?

* * *

A pharmaceutical company was conducting a survey in the suburbs of Chicago to see if their products were being purchased. The interviewer knocked on a door and asked the housewife, "Is Vaseline a product used in your home?"

"Yeah," said the woman. "We use Vaseline when we have sex. We put it on the doorknob so the kids can't get in."

* * *

Clarise and Sheffield were having a mid-afternoon breakfast. Their Park Avenue apartment was completely askew after a wild, all-night party.

"Dear, this is rather embarrassing," said Sheffield, "but was it you I made love to in the library last night?"

"About what time?" asked Clarise.

# WIFE SWAPPING

*A type of sexual fourplay*

* * *

*Add fun to your life. Try a floorsome-foursome.*

* * *

Two wives met on the street.

"You've been going around telling people there's a wart on the end of my husband's penis."

"I did *not!* I only said it *felt* like it!"

* * *

Mitford came home all excited. "Honey," he exclaimed to his wife, "I've heard about a new way to have sex, and they say it's a lot of fun. We do it back-to-back!"

"Are you nuts?" she sneered. "How can we do it back-to-back?"

"Easy," he grinned. "We invite another couple."

* * *

Melvin's wife went out of town to visit her mother for a couple of weeks. He met

126

a real cute chick at the bowling alley and sneaked home with her.

"Uh uh!" refused the girl. "Not without protection."

"Wait a mintue," moaned Melvin. "I'll get my wife's diaphragm."

After looking all over for it he came back to the pick-up. "How do you like that? She doesn't trust me!" exclaimed Melvin. "She took it with her!"

\* \* \*

Barry was complaining to his friend Fletcher. "That damned wife of mine is a liar!" he roared.

"How do you know?" asked Fletcher.

"Because she said she spent the night with Rhoda."

"So?"

"*I* spent the night with Rhoda!"

\* \* \*

*Have you heard about the husband who took a mistress just to break the monogamy?*

**Husband:** Let's go out and have some real fun tonight.

**Wife:** Okay. If you get home first, leave a light in the hall.

\* \* \*

The delectable doll was complaining to the bartender. "My husband is always away on business trips. What would you do in my place?"

"Honey," answered the bartender, "let's go over to your place and I'll show you!"

\* \* \*

"My husband must have been quite a bedroom operator before we married," confided Nora to her best friend. "Whenever there's a thunderstorm at night and lightning flashes, he bolts upright in bed and shouts, 'I'll buy the negatives!'"

\* \* \*

## A SPOUSE'S SOPHISTRY

*When a marriage starts to break up, the best thing to do is to start picking up the pieces—a piece here and a piece there.*

As the time drew near, Edna asked her obstetrician, "Will my husband be permitted to stay with me during the delivery?"

"Oh, yes," answered the physician. "I feel that the father of the child should also be present at its birth."

"I don't think that would be a very good idea," said Edna, "he and my husband don't get along too well."

\* \* \*

## HAPPY MARRIED COUPLE

*Husband out with another man's wife*

\* \* \*

Hal and Gregg were drinking together in a bar. "I screwed my wife before our wedding," said Hal. "Did you?"

"I'm not sure," said Gregg. "How long have you been married to her?"

Kathy came home with a brand-new mink coat.

"Where did you get that?" asked her husband Edward.

"I won it in a raffle," she replied.

The following night Kathy walked in with a beautiful diamond bracelet.

"Where did that come from?" asked Edward.

"I won it at a raffle," said Kathy. Then she added, "And dear, do me a favor. I'm going to another raffle party tonight and I'm in a hurry. Would you mind drawing my bath?"

Edward did as instructed but when Kathy came in to take her bath, she found that there was only a half-inch of water in the tub.

"Edward," she said, "why didn't you fill the tub?"

"Well, darling," he answered, "I didn't want you to get your raffle ticket wet!"

*"I didn't want to get your raffle ticket wet!"*

Danny discovered his wife was cheating with another guy. So he went to this guy's wife and told her about it. "I know what we'll do," she said, "let's take revenge on them."

So they went to a motel and had revenge on them.

She said, "Let's have more revenge," and they kept having revenge, revenge.

Finally, Danny said, "That's enough revenge—I have no more hard feelings."

\* \* \*

Returning home for a forgotten briefcase, the husband found his pretty wife standing naked on the bathroom scales. Not bothering to enter the room he reached in, patted her on the bottom, and asked, "How much today, baby?"

"The same as always," she answered. "Two quarts of milk and a pound of butter."

\* \* \*

"I don't really mind him being unfaithful," said the wife to the marriage counselor, "but I just *can't* sleep three in a bed."

"Darling," said the wife, "do you remember those trout you spent two weeks fishing for back in April?"

"Yeah," mumbled her husband.

"Well," she continued, "one of them called last night to say you're going to be a father."

\* \* \*

*For a married man, the only thing worse than coming home with lipstick on your collar is being caught with leg make-up on your ears.*

\* \* \*

"Say," said Goodman to the host of the party, "there's a lot of good stuff here tonight. If I find a chick who's ready, would you mind if I used your extra bedroom for a quickie?"

"Not at all," replied the gracious host, "but what about your wife?"

"Nothing to worry about," said Goodman, "I'll only be gone for a few minutes and she'll never miss me."

"No, I'm sure she won't miss you," agreed the host, "but fifteen minutes ago *she* borrowed the extra bedroom."

"I had everything a man could want," moaned Manny to his pal in the steam room. "Money, a handsome home, the love of a beautiful and wealthy woman. Then, bang, one morning my wife walked in!"

\* \* \*

## HENPECKED HUSBAND

*One who is afraid to tell his pregnant wife that he is sterile*

\* \* \*

For years, Hart and Mitchell and their respective wives had been occupying neighboring cabanas at the beach.

One day, Hart said, "Listen, how about switching? There's no need for me to be with my wife and you to be with your wife all the time."

"Hmmmm," said Mitchell, "I admit I've thought of it myself. Let's ask the girls. If they're willing, why not?"

Each consulted his wife and they seemed amenable. When cabana time came, therefore, the foursome split up so that each was not with his or her married partner.

On the morning after the first night,

Hart said to Mitchell, "How did you enjoy it?"

"I liked it," said Mitchell, "and I think we ought to continue."

"Exactly my feelings," said Hart. "Now let's go next door and see how the two girls made out!"

\*　　\*　　\*

# SENSUOUS SENIOR CITIZENS

*Spectacular Spooners * Sweet-Talking Smoochers * Snowy-Haired Seducers * Sizzling Spring Chickens*

\*　　\*　　\*

On her fiftieth wedding anniversary, the sweet little old lady was asked, "In all these years, have you ever thought of divorce?"

"My goodness no!" she replied. "I was getting all I wanted on the outside as it was!"

* * *

## OPTIMIST

*A guy who gets married at the age of 89 and starts looking for a house close to a school*

Anderson, aged 82, heard that rolls loaded with sesame seeds would help his sex life, so he went to the bakery. "Let me have $20 worth of those rolls covered with sesame seeds!"

"Twenty dollars' worth?" said the baker. "Why they'll get hard on you before you can eat 'em!"

"In that case," said the old man, "give me $40 worth!"

\* \* \*

Markowitz, a 70-year-old millionaire, just married an 18-year-old girl. His friend Shapiro said, "You're a millionaire, marrying an 18-year-old girl. How can you get a girl like that when you're 70?"

The old guy replied, "I told her I was 90."

\* \* \*

Sol and Abe, two 85-year-old widowers, were sitting on a park bench in St. Petersburg, Florida. Sol was telling Abe about a local gal that he had dated the night before.

"What did you do?" asked Abe.

"We checked into a motel, got in bed, and I sang, 'Those Were the Days.'"

"That sounds like a great evening," said Abe. "Do you mind if I take her out tonight?"

"Sure, go ahead."

The next day, Sol said, "How did it go last night?"

"Fine."

"What did you do?"

"Well, we got a motel room and got into bed. I couldn't remember the song, so I screwed her."

\* \* \*

Morgan, aged 86, was talking to his doctor. "About four weeks ago," he said, "I picked up an 18-year-old girl, took her to a motel, and we made love all night. Three weeks ago, I met a 20-year-old, double parked in front of her house, and we did it for three hours. Just last week, I grabbed a 17-year-old, took her to the park and we've been making love for six straight days."

"My goodness," gasped the doctor, "picking up all these strange girls; I hope you're using some precaution!"

"Oh, sure," said the old man, "I give them a phoney name and address."

An elderly couple went to a doctor. The man said, "We want to know if we're making love properly. Will you look at us?"

"Go ahead," said the doctor. They made love.

"You're making love perfectly," the doctor said. "That will be $10."

They came back six weeks in a row and did the same thing. On the seventh visit the doctor said, "What are you coming here like this for—I told you you're making love properly."

"She can't come to my house," said the man, "and I can't go to her house. A motel costs $20. You charge us $10 and we get $8 back from Medicare."

The 19-year-old bride had been married only three months when her 76-year-old husband died. When asked by her mother how the aged man had expired she told this story:

"We were real happy. He was a kind, gentle, generous man and a real good lover for his age. Sunday mornings were special to him and he would make love to me to the rhythm of the church bells. He'd be alive today if it wasn't for that lousy fire engine that went clanging by."

\* \* \*

*Grandpa:* Doc, you remember that pep medicine you gave me last week?
*Doctor:* Yes, what about it?
*Grandpa:* I accidentally dropped it in the well.
*Doctor:* Goodness man! You're not drinking the water, are you?
*Grandpa:* Heck, no! We can't even get the pump handle down!

\* \* \*

Eighty-year-old Douglas went to his doctor for a blood test and medical examination before getting married.

The doctor checked him over, then asked,

"You mean at your age you really want to get married?"

"Well," replied the old man. "I don't exactly want to. I've got to."

\* \* \*

An elderly gentleman visited his doctor with the complaint that he believed he was becoming impotent.

"When did you first become aware of this problem?" the doctor asked.

The old man replied, "Yesterday afternoon, twice last night, and again this morning."

\* \* \*

Silas approached his aged grandfather. "Grandpappy, you're getting pretty old and feeble," he said. "Don't you think you'd better go to the poor house?"

"You're dadburned right, sonny. I'm a rarin'. Let's get along."

"Okay, Grandpappy, but I can't understand why you're so anxious to go to the poor house."

"*Poor* house? *Poor* house? That's my mistake, youngster."

As they sat in the sun at the Retirement Villa in Daytona Beach, an old man said to his elderly companion, "Fannie, you must have had a lot of good screwing in your day."

"Yes," she replied, "but I never appreciated it as much as the little I get lately."

\* \* \*

Two stately South Carolina colonels got off a train in Charleston. Both men, dressed in long cutaway coats, had flowing white beards that came to their chests. "Well," said one to the other, "shall we check into a hotel or go directly to the whorehouse?"

\* \* \*

"What's the most useless thing on Grandma?"
"Grandpa!"

\* \* \*

## OLD TIMER'S TESTAMENT

*The enjoyment of sex (although great*
*For some years) is then said to abate.*
*It may well be so,*
*But how should I know?*
*For I'm only seventy-eight.*

Molly, aged 79, complained of abdominal swelling and pain to the doctor. He examined her thoroughly, put her through a series of laboratory tests, and then announced the results.

"The plain fact, madam," said the medical man, "is that you're pregnant."

"That's impossible!" said Molly. "Why, I'm seventy-nine years old and my husband, although he still works, is eighty-six!"

The doctor insisted, so the aging mother-to-be pulled over his desk telephone and dialed her husband's office. When he was on the line, she shouted, "You old goat, you've got me pregnant!"

"Please," quavered the old man, "who did you say was calling?"

*　　*　　*

It was midnight when the phone rang at police headquarters. The desk sergeant answered, and a shrill voice reported, "There's a sex maniac in my house."

"Try to be calm, lady," said the cop. "We'll have a patrol car there in a few minutes."

"Oh, that's not necessary," answered the caller. "Just send somebody around to pick him up in the morning."

Ninety-year-old Parker went to a bordello and was so great in bed the prostitute said, "Old man, if you can do it again, it's on the house!"

"Okay," said Parker, "but if you don't mind, I'd like to take a 15-minute nap!"

"Okay."

"And while I'm sleeping, I'd like you to hold my ding dong!"

She agreed. When he woke up, Parker gave another great performance. So the girl said, "Look, if you can handle it, I'll give you another one for free!"

He agreed, "Okay, but I gotta take another 15-minute nap and while I'm sleeping, you have to hold my knob!"

Parker woke up later and once again performed like a teenager. "Say, Pop," said the hooker, "I can understand why you want to take the 15-minute nap, but why did you want me to hold your pecker?"

"Well," said the old man, "the last place I went to, somebody stole my wallet!"

*"Somebody stole my wallet!"*

Did you hear about the old maid who took a tramp in the woods?

* * *

Before she left a friend's house, Aunt Emma was warned that a sex maniac was loose in the neighborhood. That evening, when she returned to her apartment, she cautiously looked under her bed, in her closet, and behind the draperies.

Then Emma switched on the light. "Well, he's not here!" she sighed. "Damn it!"

* * *

When the old maid surprised a teenage burglar in her boudoir, he pleaded, "Let me go, lady. I never did anything wrong before."

"Well," she leered, "you look big enough to learn."

* * *

*An eccentric old spinster called Lowell*
*Announced to her friends, "Bless my*
*sowell*
*I've gained so much weight*
*I am sorry to state*
*I fear that I'm going to fowell."*

"Just a minute, young man!" said the spinster to the obscene phone caller. "I want to get a cup of coffee and a cigarette."

*　*　*

## TRULY DESPERATE SPINSTER

*One who leaves food on the back porch for Peeping Toms*

*　*　*

The other night when an old maid found a tramp under her bed, it so upset her that her stomach was on the bum all night.

*　*　*

The patient whose history card a doctor was filling out said she was a spinster. So, when he came to the space for listing number of children, he automatically put down "none."

"But, Doctor," she said, "I have a 13-year-old daughter."

"I thought you told me you were an old maid?" he said.

"I am," she replied. "But I'm not a stubborn old maid."

The woman phoned down to the hotel manager. "I'm up here in room 1510," she shouted angrily, "and I want you to know there is a man walking around in the room across the way with not one stitch of clothes on and his shades are up."

"I'll send the house detective up right away, madam," said the manager.

The detective entered the woman's room, peered across the way, and said, "You're right, madam, the man hasn't any clothes on, but his window sill covers him from the waist down no matter where he is in his room."

"Indeed?" yelped the lady. "Stand on the bed! Stand on the bed!"

\* \* \*

Martha, a middle-aged spinster, returned to her apartment with a supply of birth-control pills she'd just purchased at the local pharmacy. "I don't understand it," said her roommate. "In the past three weeks you've purchased enough birth-control pills to last a year, plus vaginal foam, flavored douches, and a diaphragm—and I didn't even know you had a boyfriend. Who are you trying to seduce?"

"I should think you could guess," said the woman. "The druggist."

Lizzie and Iona, two old maids in Arkansas, were rocking on the porch of their farmhouse.

"Say," said Lizzie to her friend, "let's go down to the cucumber patch and do pushups!"

\* \* \*

*A desperate spinster named Clare*
*Once knelt in the moonlight all bare*
*And prayed to her God*
*"Take me here on the sod."*
*Then a passerby answered her prayer.*

\* \* \*

Two robbers broke into a bank in a small town. "All right," said the bigger man. "Line up! We're gonna rob all the men and rape all the women!"

"Wait a second," snapped his partner. "Let's just grab the dough and beat it!"

"Shut up and mind your own business," said the spinster from behind the counter. "The big fella knows what he's doing!"

\* \* \*

Grandpa Buford is 94 and boasts that he makes love to three women a day. Recently, though, he sadly admits, he's had to caution them not to cough.

The town grocer gave his beautiful teenage daughter Jenny a job as clerk in his store. Soon the local wolves began dropping by requesting items stocked on the highest shelves, because each time Jenny climbed up a ladder to fill their orders, they were assured a spectacular view.

Naive as she was attractive, Jenny didn't catch on. She rearranged the stock, but no matter how she planned it, the boys always seemed to ask for the items she put at the top.

One day an elderly gent entered the store while a bunch of these youngsters was sending poor Jenny up and down the ladder. Each boy ordered a loaf of raisin bread from the top shelf. On her fifth climb she hoped to save an additional trip, so Jenny called down to the senior citizen, "Is yours raisin, too?"

"Nope," said the oldtimer. "But it's twitchin' a mite."

\*     \*     \*

Two little old ladies were chatting over the backyard fence. The first one boasted, "I went out with old man Cain last night, and I had to slap him twice."

"To stop him?" asked her friend.

"No," she giggled. "To start him."

\*     \*     \*

As they sunned on the park bench, one

senior citizen told another, "It's been so long since I had any, I can't remember for sure whether I ever did or not."

*   *   *

Old Lindley sat down at the doctor's desk.

"What is your problem?" asked the physician.

"Well, doc, after the first, I'm very tired. After the second, I feel all in. After the third, my hearts begins to pound. After the fourth, I break out in a cold sweat. And after the fifth, I'm so exhausted, I feel I could die!"

"Incredible!" said the M.D. "How old are you?"

"Seventy-six."

"Well, at seventy-six, don't you think you should stop after the first?"

"But doctor, how can I stop after the first when I live on the fifth?"

*   *   *

She lay in bed, blissfully happy on this, the first morning of her long-dreamed-of honeymoon. "Darling," she called as she heard him puttering around in the bathroom. "Did you brush your teeth yet?"

"Yes," he cooed. "And while I was at it, I brushed yours, too."

Max, aged 76, upon returning to his apartment late one night, was startled to find a girl of about 18 ransacking the place.

"Young woman, you are a thief!" he said. "I'm going to call the police."

"Mister," she pleaded, "if I'm arrested again, I'll be sent away for years. Please don't call the police."

"I'm sorry, but I have to do it!" Max replied.

"Look," she cried, "I'll do anything. I'll give you my body."

"Okay," said the senior citizen, "take off your clothes and get in bed."

The girl did and Max quickly followed. He tried and tried and tried for about twenty minutes. Exhausted and in defeat, he finally gave up.

"It's no use," sighed Max. "I just can't make it. I'll have to call the police."

To celebrate their fortieth anniversary, Seymour and Rose went back to the same second-floor hotel room where they had spent their honeymoon.

"Now," said Seymour, "just like that first night, let's undress, get in opposite corners of the room, turn off the lights, then run to each other and embrace."

They undressed, went to opposite corners, switched out the lights and ran towards each other. But their sense of direction was dulled by forty years, so Seymour missed Rose and he went right through the window.

He landed on the lawn in a daze. Seymour tapped on the lobby window to get the clerk's attention. "I fell down from upstairs," he said. "I'm naked and I gotta get back to my room."

"It's okay," said the clerk. "Nobody'll see you."

"Are you crazy? I gotta walk through the lobby and I'm all naked!"

"Nobody can see you," repeated the clerk. "Everybody's upstairs trying to get some old lady off a doorknob!"

\* \* \*

# BAWDY BEASTS

*Brutish Beavers * Bestial Bears *
Brazen Bulls * Bolk Billy Goats *
Balmy Buzzards * Bisexual
Bumblebees*

*     *     *

"No," cried the girl centipede crossing her legs, "a thousand times, no!"

\*     \*     \*

Two small mice were crouched under a table in the show girls' dressing room of a big Las Vegas night spot.

"Wow," exclaimed the first mouse, "have you ever seen so many gorgeous legs in your life?"

"Means nothing to me," said the second, "I'm a titmouse."

Said the nanny goat to the billy goat:
"You can go as far as you want to, tall,
dark and stinky! Just don't kid me!"

\* \* \*

*The dairy maid put on her coat*
  *To go and milk the family goat*
*She tried and tried and then she cried,*
  *"Oh, Nanny, you be still."*
*Nanny tried and then replied,*
  *"This ain't Nanny, this is Bill."*

\* \* \*

Where does the bumblebee keep his
stinger at night?
In his honey.

\* \* \*

Once upon a time there was a boy penguin and a girl penguin who met at the
equator. After a brief but charming inter-
lude, the boy penguin went north to the
North Pole and the girl pengiun went
south to the South Pole.

Later a telegram arrived at the North
Pole stating simply: COME QUICK I AM
WITH BYRD.

"Grrr," said the wolf, leaping at Little Red Riding Hood, "I'm going to eat you!"

"For God's sake," Red replied. "Doesn't anybody screw anymore?"

*   *   *

A performing octopus could play the piano, the zither, and the piccolo. His trainer wanted him to add the bagpipe to his accomplishments, so he placed the Scottish instrument in the octopus' room.

Hours passed, but no bagpipe music was heard. The trainer was disturbed. The next morning he anxiously asked the eight-tentacled creature, "Have you learned to play that thing yet?"

*"Play it?"* replied the octopus. "I've been trying to *lay* it all night!"

*   *   *

## EMASCULATED DINOSAUR

*A colossal fossil with a docile tassel*

*   *   *

"How do porcupines have sex?"
"Carefully, very carefully."

Two elderly farmers were strolling through a pasture when one stopped and remarked, "Here's where I got my first piece, and right over there's where her mother stood."

"Her mother!" cried the other farmer. "What did she say?"

"Ba-a-a-a-a," came the reply.

\* \* \*

A woman visiting the Bronx Zoo sidled up to the wire netting, and began petting the kangaroo very gently. Then for some unknown reason she slid her hand down the kangaroo's back, grabbed hold of its genitals and squeezed.

The kangaroo leaped in the air, hopped over the eight-foot fence, and went racing across the zoo.

Immediately, the zookeeper ran up to the woman, pulled down his pants and said, "Lady, squeeze mine too. I've gotta go catch that son-of-a-bitch."

\* \* \*

A little boy and girl squirrel were chattering and playing around when suddenly a fox appeared. The girl squirrel dashed up a tree but the boy squirrel stayed on the ground.

"That's strange," said the fox. "Usually squirrels are afraid of me and run up the nearest tree."

"Listen," said the boy squirrel. "Did you ever try to climb a tree after playing with a girl for twenty minutes?"

\* \* \*

A squirrel on the ground was watching two other squirrels in a tree. One of them fell to the ground, bounced a couple of times—looked back up in the tree and said, "That making love in the tree is for the birds."

\* \* \*

Luke won a live duck in a barroom drawing, and wandered into a theater carrying it. He was told he couldn't bring the duck in with him, so he went away and hid it inside his pants.

In the darkened theater the woman sitting next to him clutched her escort's sleeve and whispered, "The man next to me has his dong out."

"So what?" said her boyfriend. "You've seen one before."

"But this one is eating popcorn!"

A woodpecker came to Texas from another state and was up a tree pecking away. While doing this, lightning struck the tree splitting it down the middle.

"It beats hell how hard your pecker can get when you're away from home," he said.

\* \* \*

Once during a severe rain storm, three roosters found themselves caught in the deluge. Two of them ran for the barn. The third, and smartest one, made a duck under the porch.

\* \* \*

What has the shortest sex life?
An egg. It's laid once and eaten once.

\* \* \*

*Am I a people?*
*No, you are a chicken.*
*Do chickens come from people?*
*No, chickens come from eggs.*
*Are eggs born?*
*No, eggs are laid.*
*Are people laid?*
*No, some people are chicken.*

# THE HEIGHT OF CONCEIT

*A flea, floating down the river
with an erection, whistling for
the drawbridge to open*

\* \* \*

Three little chickens had dates for the evening. When they got back to their hen house, they compared notes. "I had a great time," said the first. "I had a Plymouth Rock for a partner and we rocked all evening."

"I had a great time, too," chirped the second. "I went out with a Rhode Island Red and he showed me how to paint the town."

"What sort of a date did you have?" they asked the third hen.

"Terrible," she sighed. "I was stuck with a capon who did nothing but talk about his operation all night."

\* \* \*

Did you hear about the gay parakeet who had a compulsion to kiss a cockatoo every day?

When a recently bought rooster died after only three weeks on the job, Farmer Foster was determined that its replacement would last much longer. So before putting the new rooster to work, Foster dosed it heavily with vitamins and pep pills.

The instant the bird was released, it charged into the hen coop and serviced every one of the hens.

Then it flew into the adjoining coop and proceeded to do the same for the geese.

Farmer Foster went back to the house, shaking his head and muttering, "He'll never last out the day."

Around sunset, Foster was crossing the yard, and there lay the rooster, legs aloft, flat on its back, with two hungry buzzards slowly circling above.

"Damn it!" groaned Foster. "Now I've got to buy me *another* new rooster!"

The rooster opened one eye, winked, and pointed at the nearing buzzards, saying, "Shhh!"

*"Shhh!"*

Three men from Texas were hurt in an airplane crash in Africa and were recuperating in a Moroccan hospital. In Morocco, they allow the shepherds to bring their flocks into town to graze, which helps to keep the grass short.

One day, the Americans, confined to their hospital rooms for several months, looked out a window. There was a flock of sheep enjoying lunch. The first Texan pointed to a plump ewe and exclaimed, "I wish that one was Elizabeth Taylor!"

"I wish that was Raquel Welch!" said another.

"I just wish it was dark!" said the third man.

\* \* \*

Every morning Farmer Wilkins put his pig in a wheelbarrow in order to take it to his friend's farm for mating. He did this for several weeks.

After three months the farmer's wife went to the pigpen to see if the pig had shown any symptoms. When she returned her husband asked, "Well, is she?"

"No," Mrs. Wilkins answered, "but the pig is waiting in the wheelbarrow."

Why can't a baby duck lay eggs?
The quack's too small.

\* \* \*

"I'm in love with my horse," said Andrew to the psychiatrist.

"That's nothing," replied the shrink. "A lot of people love animals. My wife and I have a dog that we love very much."

"Ah, but doctor, it's a physical attraction that I feel toward my horse!"

"Ummmm!" said the analyst. "What kind of horse is it? Male or female?"

"Female, of course!" said Andrew. "What do you think I am, queer?"

\* \* \*

Did you hear about the farmer who had a nervous breakdown?

Seems he tried to take inventory on a rabbit farm.

\* \* \*

As one rabbit said to another, "You've had it."

171

Two rabbits were being chased by a pack of dogs, when one turned to the other and said, "What are we running for? Let's stop and outnumber them."

"Keep running," said the other rabbit. "Keep running, we're brothers."

* * *

*It is the unfortunate habit*
*Of the rabbit to breed like a rabbit.*
*One can say without question*
*This leads to congestion*
*In the burrows that rabbits inhabit.*

* * *

While on their honeymoon, Kit and Netty bought a talkative parrot and took it back to their hotel room. As they made love the bird kept up a running commentary. Finally, Kit flung a bath towel over the cage and said, "If you don't shut up I'm sending you to the zoo!"

Getting ready to leave the following morning, they couldn't close a bulging suitcase and decided one of them would stand on it while the other attempted to fasten it.

"Darling," said Kit, "you get on top and I'll try." That didn't work. So he said, "Now I'll get on top and you try." That didn't work either. "Look," said Kit, "let's both get on top and try."

The parrot yanked away the towel and said, "Zoo or no zoo, this I've gotta see!"

\* \* \*

*There was an old bachelor of Ware*
*Who had an affair with a bear,*
*  He explained, "I don't mind,*
*  For it's gentle and kind,*
*But I wish it had slightly less hair."*

\* \* \*

Mama bear took her little baby cubs out to play in the backyard. She watched them as they tmubled around on the grass, playing the games that all baby bears do. Suddenly the little girl bear came running and asked:

"Mommy, when I grow up and get married, will I have a little baby bear?"

Little brother came running over and asked his mother:

"Mommy, when I grow up and get married, will I have a little baby bear, too?"

"No dear," replied Mama.

"Why?"

"Because you have no little cubby hole."

A farmer who had only two impotent old bulls bought a new, young, vigorous bull. Immediately, the stud began mounting one cow after another in the pasture. After watching this for an hour, one of the ancient bulls started pawing the ground and snorting.

"What's the matter?" asked the other. "You getting young ideas?"

"No," said the first bull, "but I don't want that young fellow to think I'm one of the cows."

\* \* \*

Reid was very fond of his male parrot. The parrot had become despondent and after all sorts of experiments to snap him out of it, Reid decided that his feathered friend needed some sex.

Reid found a beautiful female parrot in a pet shop and paid $50 to have his bird serviced.

The female was delivered to Reid's house and placed in the male parrot's cage. Instantly the male let out a terrifying scream and began tearing the female's feathers out.

"What are you doing?" screeched the female.

"For fifty bucks, Baby," shouted the male, "I want you nude."

The circus had finished its final performance in the country town when one of its zebras took sick. The local veterinarian suggested rest for the beast, so the circus owner made arrangements to board it at a nearby farm.

The zebra took to the new life by meeting all the animals of the barnyard.

He came across a chicken and said, "I'm a zebra, who are you?"

"I'm a chicken," said the chicken.

"What do you do?" asked the zebra.

"I scratch around and lay eggs."

The zebra walked up to a cow. "I'm a zebra. Who are you?"

"I'm a cow," said the cow.

"What do you do?" asked the zebra.

"I graze in the field and give milk."

The zebra met a bull next. "I'm a zebra," he said. "Who are you?"

"I'm a bull."

"And what do you do?" asked the zebra.

"What do I do!" snorted the bull. "Why you silly looking ass—take off your pajamas and I'll show you!"

\* \* \*

Phillip phoned Shirley to invite her out for a lamb dinner.

"What do you mean, a lamb dinner?" asked Shirley, somewhat puzzled.

"Three cocktails and a piece of ewe," smirked Phillip.

175

"It was deep in the woods back yonder," began old Herbie, the guide. "I was plodding along minding my own business when suddenly a huge bear sneaked up behind me. He pinned my arms to my sides and started to squeeze the breath out of me. My gun fell out of my hands. First thing you know, the bear had stooped down, picked up the gun, and was pressing it against my back."

"What did you do?" gasped the tenderfoot.

Old Herbie sighed. "What could I do? I married his daughter."

# TAXIDERMIST

*A man who mounts animals*

\* \* \*

Old Mrs. Morris, who lived in a small Southern town, had two pet monkeys, Tom and Dick, that she loved very much.

One day Tom took sick and died. A couple of days later Dick died of a broken heart.

Wanting to keep them, the kindly old lady took them to an animal stuffer.

"Do you want them mounted?" he asked.

"Oh, no," she replied, "just have them holding hands."

\* \* \*

Sally strolled through the zoo and finally stopped in front of the deserted monkey island.

"Where are all the monkeys today?" she asked the zoo keeper.

"They're back in the cave, miss; it's the mating season."

"Will they come out if I throw them some peanuts?"

"I don't know," said the keeper. "Would you?"

Complaining of the distance between campus buildings, Velma, the veterinarian's daughter, wrote home for money to buy a bicycle. But by the time the money arrived, she'd changed her mind and bought a monkey instead. After a few weeks, the animal began losing its hair. Hoping her father might know a cure, Velma wrote: "All the hair is falling off my monkey—what shall I do?"

Her father sent this telegram:
SELL THE BICYCLE!

*   *   *

# COLLEGIATE COHABITATORS

*Catty Coeds * Cuckholded Coaches*
Chaste Cheerleaders * Campus
Carnalizers * Classmate Copulators *
Cunning-Linguists*

*       *       *

The Syracuse sorority sexpot and her boyfriend were in the throes of passionate love when the telephone rang.

"Answer the phone," said the guy.

"You answer it yourself," said the girl. "It's at your end!"

\* \* \*

*Said a pretty young student from*
    *Smith*
*Whose virtue was largely a myth,*
    *"Try hard as I can,*
    *I can't find a man*
*Whom it's fun to be virtuous with."*

The Columbia cutie returned to the sorority house after her first breakfast date at a neighboring fraternity with her steady boyfriend. Asked what she had, she replied, "Him and eggs."

* * *

As their car stopped on the shoulder of a secluded road, the handsome West Pointer asked his date, "If I try to make love to you, will you yell for help?"

"Well," said the Cornell coed, "only if you really need it."

* * *

"That was the dullest party I've ever been to," complained the California campus cutie to her roommate. "God, was I bored."

"But you stayed quite a while, didn't you?" asked her roommate.

"Yes—but only because I couldn't find my clothes."

* * *

Reminiscing with her dorm roommate about their childhood, the sweet young thing asked, "Did you ever play with jacks?"

"Oh, yes," replied her roomie. "And with Tommy's, Bill's, and Freddy's."

\* \* \*

## SIGN IN A SOPHOMORE'S PAD

*I Never Made a Man I Didn't Like*

\* \* \*

"Tell me all about the party you went to last night," begged Emily, the Northwestern coed, of her roommate Joanne.

"It was great," said Joanne. "Everybody drank gin and then they turned out the lights and I got laid twice."

"Twice?" squealed Emily.

"Yeah, twice," said Joanne. "Once by the football team and once by the track team!"

\* \* \*

*There was a young coed named Lynn*
*Who thought fornication a sin,*
*But when she was tight,*
*It seemed quite all right,*
*So everyone filled her with gin.*

The pretty coed nervously asked the doctor to perform an unusual operation—the removal of a large chunk of green wax from her naval. Looking up from the ticklish task, the physician asked, "How did this happen?"

"Well, you see, doc," said the girl, "my boyfriend likes to eat by candlelight."

\* \* \*

Doctor Bieber was perplexed by the case at hand. He had given the sorority girl all sorts of tests, but his results were still inconclusive.

"I'm not sure what it is," he finally admitted. "You either have a cold or you're pregnant."

"I must be pregnant," said the girl, "I don't know anybody who could have given me a cold."

\* \* \*

*It was hard on Wilbur trying to keep up with his classmates at the military academy. But when he transferred to a coeducational high school, it got even harder.*

\* \* \*

"Hey, Edith, how come you're not wearing my fraternity pin?"

"It was such a nuisance. All the guys were complaining that it scratched their hands."

* * *

During a wild fraternity party, Ned noticed a very prim and pretty girl sitting quietly apart from the noisy crowd. He approached her and introduced himself, then said, "I'm afraid you and I don't really fit in with this jaded group. Why don't I take you home?"

"Okay," said the girl. "Where do you live?

* * *

It was in an adult-education math course that the instructor asked the class, "If a man sold a dozen diamond necklaces at seventy-five thousand dollars apiece and his profit was twenty-five percent, what would he get for himself?"

One student raised her hand. "Anything he asked me for," she sighed.

* * *

*Cheerleader:* I love you in the worst way!
*Grid Star:* Not quite . . . you're better than a few I've had.

The Senior Prom was in full swing at a western university. Boyd, the basketball star, had finally gotten Greta alone on the country club verandah.

They sat together on a swing, when suddenly Greta's steady beau appeared on the scene, finding them locked in a tight embrace.

"I don't mind you necking with my girl," he remarked caustically, "but get your hand the hell off my fraternity pin!"

*"Get your hand off my
fraternity pin!"*

Barbi, a Bennington beauty, telephoned her mother that she had broken her engagement when her fiancé admitted that he had had affairs with two other girls in the dorm.

"But a girl can't always expect to be the first, dear," comforted her mother. "Some men deliberately seek experience before marriage for the sake of their brides-to-be."

"I know," sobbed Barbi, "but I made Matthew tell me the others' names, and everything they know about sex, they learned from *me!*"

\* \* \*

Susan, a Sarah Lawrence soph, approached her mother at Easter, eyes filled with tears. "Mom," she confessed, "I'm pregnant."

"Ye Gods!" screamed her mother. "Who is the father?"

"How should I know?" she wailed. "You never would let me go steady."

\* \* \*

*"Far dearer to me than my treasure,"*
*Miss Martingale said, "is my leisure.*
*For then I can screw*
*The whole Harvard crew—*
*They're slow, but it lengthens the*
*pleasure."*

The lovely school swimming champ was amorously engaged when her bedside phone rang one evening. Since she'd been waiting for a talk-show call, she answered it. "I'm the sports director of the YWCA," the caller said, "and I was wondering if someone in your position could possibly teach our youngsters the proper swimming techniques."

"I'm sorry," moaned the girl, "but anyone in my position would drown!"

\* \* \*

*There was a young coed of Norwood*
*Whose ways were provokingly*
    *forward.*
  *Said her mother, "My dear,*
  *You wiggle, I fear,*
*Your posterior just like a*
    *whorewood."*

\* \* \*

Tyler and Maureen met at a fraternity dance, and an hour later were parked in lovers' lane, cementing their new relationship. Tyler had freed Maureen of blouse and bra, and was removing the rest of her clothing when a police car drove by.

"Fuzz," he whispered.

"What did you expect," she replied, "a ponytail?"

191

Statistics show that Yale grads have 1.3 children, while Vassar grads have 1.7. Which merely goes to show that women have more children than men.

*   *   *

Cheerleader: It's shameful the way you start making passes at me after a half-dozen drinks.
Football Hero: What's shameful about that?
Cheerleader: The waste of five drinks.

*   *   *

Biff was the strong, silent type. He walked into the school cafeteria, ordered coffee, and winked at the waitress, a sensuous blue-eyed senior. She smiled.

"Want to go riding?" he asked.

"Sure, I'll be ready in five minutes."

So they got in the car and he drove out on the highway. Then he took off down a road. Then he drove down a lane. The lane came to a dead end and he stopped the car and cut the motor off.

Turning to her, he uttered his first speech. "Well, howaboutit?"

The waitress nodded. "Okay," she said. "You've out-talked me!"

*　　*　　*

It was a blind date, but Avery the fraternity president really wanted to impress Patti, the pretty frosh. They had dinner with champagne, saw a play, went dancing . . . and then wound up at his apartment for soft music, candlelight and more wine.

"Just how," asked Patti from the couch, "did Tim describe me in setting up our date?"

"Well—er," began Avery, "he told me you were pretty in a perky way, were an excellent conversationalist, had an attention-getting figure . . ."

"But he didn't" broke in Patti as she undid his zipper, "say anything about my being a pushover?"

*　　*　　*

## SIGN IN CAMPUS MEN'S DORMITORY

*Help Stamp Out VD*
*Use Your Head*

*There was a young coed at Kent*
*Who said that she knew what it meant*
*When studs asked her to dine*
*Upon lobster and wine.*
*She knew. Oh, she knew! But she went.*

\* \* \*

Sue and Barbara, two sexy Smith sopho-mores, were having lunch. "I dropped my pills," explained Sue, "because I was scared of the side effects."

"I still take mine," said Barbara, " 'cause I'm afraid of the front effects."

\* \* \*

## SORORITY SISTER

*A college girl who hopes to*
*graduate with a MAGNA CUM LAD*

\* \* \*

Everyone looked up as the couple walked through the restaurant to their table. She was a voluptuous phys-ed major while he was old, haggard, and stooped.

The waiter came over to take their order and the young woman proceeded to ask for the most expensive dishes in the house. Her escort was somewhat staggered and asked, "Do you eat this well at the dorm?"

"No," she replied, "but then no one there wants to sleep with me!"

\* \* \*

*There was a young girl from Penn*
*  State*
*Who stuttered when out on a date*
*  By the time she cried, "S-s-s-stop!"*
*  Or called for a c-c-c-cop*
*It was often a wee bit too late.*

\* \* \*

Helene was filing a report with the campus police on her encounter with an exhibitionist.

"Those nuts always seem to bother the nicest, most innocent girls," said one officer. "I'm real sorry you were exposed to this experience."

"Oh, that's all right," giggled the undergrad. "It was really no big thing."

\* \* \*

## SORORITY HOUSE

*An institute of lower yearning in*
*an institute of higher learning*

According to a recent poll of college students, the biggest lies on campus are:

1. God is dead
2. I was only holding the reefer for a friend
3. I'm glad you made me wait till after the wedding.

\* \* \*

"And this," said Marcus, who was showing Pete, his new college roommate, around the campus, "is our lovers' lane. The students refer to it as Firestone Drive."

"I suppose the name is related to 'hot rocks,'" said Pete.

"Not really," said Marcus. "It's called that because it's where the rubber meets the road."

\* \* \*

Bobbie Jo, a truly homely gal, came home from the Georgia campus for summer vacation. One evening she calmly confessed to her mother that she lost her virginity last semester. "How did it happen?" gasped the parent.

"Well, it wasn't easy," admitted Bobbie Jo, "but three of my sorority sisters helped hold him down!"

Norman lay naked on the grass in a secluded part of the park, a dazed but oddly happy expression on his face. "What happened?" asked the cop.

"I was—uh—minding my own business," mumbled the man, "when a gang of sorority girls from Vassar came along and jumped me and—uh—tore off my clothes. And then . . ."

"And then what?"

"And then all heaven broke loose!"

\*　　\*　　\*

Dorothy Parker, renowned for her acerbic wit, reported on a Yale University prom:

"If all those sweet young things present were laid end to end, I wouldn't be at all surprised!"

\*　　\*　　\*

Phoebe phoned home from Boston College and when her mother answered, she said, "Mother, I'm not phoning from my dorm. I'm in Ron's apartment. And prepare yourself for a shock! We're engaged!"

"For heaven's sake . . . in what?"

"Don't you know, young lady," said the irate policeman, "that two-piece bathing suits are not allowed on this beach?"

"All right, officer," replied the well-built miss, "which piece would you like me to remove?"

*"Which piece would you like me to remove?"*

"It's really true," exclaimed the satisfied soph to the star fullback beside her. "Nice guys finish last."

\* \* \*

During the spring get-together at Fort Lauderdale, a college student was arrested for indecent exposure in a field near the beach.

"I plead not guilty, Your Honor," he told the court. "I went there only to get relieved."

"I'm inclined to accept your explanation," rejoined the judge, "since there must be some allowances made for emergencies."

"That's all well and good, Your Honor," interjected the arresting officer, "but what about the young lady who relieved him?"

\* \* \*

*Up in Cambridge, Lib Cliffies discard*
*Any pretense of being on guard.*
*Though the Harvards deny it,*
*Their saltpeter diet*
*Makes it hard to get hard in the Yard.*

\* \* \*

A campus biggie went out for the first time with the vivacious little baton-twirling champion of the college marching band, and he ended up in the hospital. "What happened, Joe?" inquired his visiting roommate.

"Let's call it a case of overreaction," groaned the patient. "After the dance and a hamburger, we drove over and parked in back of the stadium. Things were going along nice, then she began to give me a real slow, hot hand job—but then some jerk in the car alongside began to whistle the school fight song!"

\*   \*   \*

*A college girl's mind moves her ahead, while a chorus girl's mind moves her behind.*

\*   \*   \*

Abby, a well-stacked coed, was undressing when her roommate, Jean, said, "Do you know there's the impression of a large M on your stomach?"

"My fiancé's in town this weekend," confided Abby, "and he likes to make love with his football-letter sweater on."

"Which school does he attend, Michigan or Minnesota?" questioned Jean.

"Neither," giggled Abby. "He goes to Wisconsin."

Hank and Buck, two UCLA buddies, had been dating the same girl and were comparing notes over a beer.

"All I've been able to do so far is kiss her good night," admitted Hank.

"Tell me," asked Buck, "when you kissed her, did she say anything about letting you do more?"

"She may have," said Hank, "but I wasn't hearing too well. Her thighs were covering my ears."

\* \* \*

*"I'll tell you," smiled prom chairman
   Mose,*
*"Why Hatty's the prom queen I chose:
   She's as cheerfully free
   As the wind on the sea
And besides, like the wind, Hatty
   blows!"*

\* \* \*

Claire and Anita, two Ohio State frosh, were discussing plans for their summer vacations. "I don't know about you," said Claire, "but I'm going to Monaco for the Grand Prix."

"I'm afraid you're in for an awful letdown," remarked Anita. "For one thing, that's not even the way it's pronounced."

Jim finally got up the nerve to speak to the pretty blonde sitting beside him in English class.

"Do you enjoy cocktails?"

"I certainly do," she replied. "Heard any good ones?"

\* \* \*

"I'm beat," confessed the pretty cheerleader to her roommate. "Last night I didn't fall asleep until after three."

"No wonder you're tired," replied her roommate. "Twice is usually all I need."

\* \* \*

An old grad was visiting his son in the newly mixed dormitories. The boy regaled him with graphic sex stories about a campus stud who happened to occupy the adjoining room.

The smiling father shook his head in disbelief. Then suddenly, small sounds began coming through the wall. Soon, it built into intense female moaning and groaning.

"By God, you're right!" exclaimed the father. "That guy must really be putting it to some girl!"

"No, Dad!" said the son, "at this point he's just *showing* it to her!"

203

One morning at coffee the three sorority sisters were considering what kind of man they'd prefer being shipwrecked with on a desert island.

"I'd want a fellow who was a wonderful conversationalist," said the first.

"That would be nice," said the second, "but I'd rather have a guy who knew how to hunt and could cook the things he caught."

The third smiled and said, "I'd settle for a good obstetrician."

\* \* \*

*Billie:* What are you doing with that letter on your sweater? Don't you know you're not supposed to wear that unless you've made the team?

*Millie:* Well?

\* \* \*

The captain of the football team walked into the athletic office to see the coach.

"Would you like to tell me your problem?" the pretty student receptionist asked. "I'll need the information for your school record."

"It's rather embarrassing," the athlete

stammered. "You see, I have a very large and almost constant erection."

"Well, the coach is very busy today," she cooed, "but maybe I can squeeze you in."

\* \* \*

*There was a young lady of Exeter*
*So pretty that men craned their necks*
*at her.*
*One was even so brave*
*As to take out and wave*
*The distinguishing mark of his sex at*
*her.*

\* \* \*

History Prof Porter was a car nut. He liked to keep his auto clean and brightly polished and so he got into the habit of using his wife's worn-out panties to polish the car. One Sunday morning he went rummaging through the rag bag but couldn't find any.

The next day at the office he said to his student stenographer, "What do you do with your panties when you wear them out?"

"Well," blushed the coed, "if I can find them afterwards, I put them in my purse."

The anthropology professor had a repu-
tation for using rough language and telling bawdy stories in class. Naturally, his
class contained few coeds. The girls who
did attend his lectures, however, were sub-
jected to his regular habit of dispensing
lewd, lockerroom humor.

They decided the time had come to do
something. Next time the professor began
his nonsense, all the girls would get up immediately, leave the classroom, and go
straight to the dean's office. Good strategy.
But the professor had been tipped off and
was ready for them.

Next morning, as soon as the class settled in, he pointed to a map of Africa and
said, "The men here have penises that are
ten inches long!"

The coeds got up and started for the
door.

"Oh, don't rush off now, girls. The boat
doesn't leave for a week."

Theresa was taking an anatomy course in an Eastern medical school. The professor asked her to go to the blackboard and draw a picture of the male sexual organ in its normal position.

She went to the board and drew a very obvious erection. "I told you to draw it in the normal position," berated the professor.

"Yes," said the girl, "but that's the only way I've ever seen one!"

\*　　\*　　\*

Student: I hear the Board of Trustees is trying to stop sex.

Coed: Is that so? First thing you know they'll be trying to make the students stop, too.

\*　　\*　　\*

Having escorted Vivian, a Vanderbilt soph, home from their first date, shy Sylvester was invited in for a nightcap. As Vivian fixed the drinks, Sylvester strolled about, a bit ill at ease, admiring her apartment.

"Be careful if you sit on that couch," said the sexy soph. "If you press down on the arm and pull forward on the seat while pushing against the back cushion, it turns into a bed."

*At Wellesley, Vassar, and Smith,*
*A common and recurring myth*
  *That a masculine member*
  *Helps students remember*
*Was found without substance or pith.*

\*     \*     \*

"Mom," asked Alene, the Alabama anatomy major, "remember when you told me the way to a man's heart was through his stomach?"

"Yes, dear," answered the mother.

"Well," said Alene, "last night I found a new route."

\*     \*     \*

In an English Lit course, the current author of discussion was Henry Miller. The professor requested an attractive but not overly bright coed to explain the difference between fornication and adultery.

"Well," she stammered, "I've tried them both, and they seem about the same."

\*     \*     \*

After several unsuccessful advances, the Penn State sophomore asked his pretty but standoffiish date, "Do you shrink from making love?"

"If I did," she sighed, "I'd be a midget."

A pretty coed had been receiving obscene phone calls from the same man for months. She was beginning to enjoy it. One night she picked up the phone and it was him again.

"I'm gonna come over there, throw you down on the bed, rip off your clothes, spread your legs, and shove something into you you'll never forget!"

"Come on over!" said the girl.

"What?" answered a surprised voice.

"I'm serious! You turn me on!"

Twenty minutes later the phone nut was in her apartment. Within five minutes they had their clothes off and within ten *seconds* the guy was all finished. To add insult to injury, he rolled over and went to sleep on the poor frustrated girl.

An hour later, he got up, dressed and headed for the door. "I'll say one thing about you," snapped the coed, "you give great phone!"

\*  \*  \*

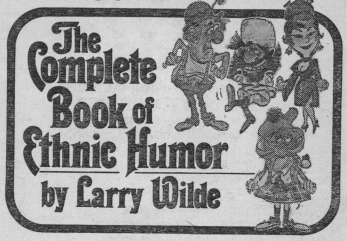

# More Best-Selling Fiction from Pinnacle

# THE LONE RANGER

## Come, return with us again to those glorious days of yesteryear!
## More bestselling western adventure from Pinnacle, America's #1 series publisher!